C U B A
Five Hundred Years
of Images

CUBA
Five Hundred Years of Images

JORGE GUILLERMO

PHOTOGRAPHS BY BRYNN BRUYN

ABARIS BOOKS

NEW YORK

THOTH PUBLISHERS

AMSTERDAM

Illustration on page one:
Window on the Church of the Holy Trinity in Santiago de Cuba.

Illustration on frontispiece:
The statue of Spanish King Ferdinand VII
that used to occupy the center of Havana's Plaza de Armas.
It was replaced after independence.

Copyright © 1992 Jorge Guillermo · Photography © 1992 Brynn Bruyn

Cover design by Richard van den Dool
Typography by Joost van de Woestijne
Color separation and printing by Craft Print, Singapore

First published in Europe and Japan by

Thoth Publishers, P. C. Hooftstraat 57¹, 1071 BN Amsterdam
The Netherlands

First published in North and South America by

Abaris Books, 42 Memorial Plaza, Pleasantville, N.Y. 10570

ISBN 90–6868–050–1   ISBN 0–89835–324–6
Thoth Publishers   Abaris Books

Foreword

THE WRITING OF this book was undertaken to mark the five hundredth anniversary of the first arrival of the Spanish in Cuba. For a number of years, Christopher Columbus has been the subject of spirited debate among historians. Various attempts have been made to prove that other navigators had found their way across the ocean before him. Serious questions have been raised about the morality of the European presence in the New World.

It is nearsighted to judge incidents that took place centuries ago according to the cultural and moral standards of our own time. Fortunately, my purpose in writing this book has not been to pass judgement, but rather the simpler one of presenting the long and fascinating line of events that have shaped the history of my native land.

I dedicate my efforts to my three children, Bernardo, Nicolás and Juliana, in the hope that they will derive as much satisfaction and pride from learning Cuba's history as I have.

Jorge Guillermo

Contents

CHAPTER ONE

Cuba Before Columbus

BEFORE COLUMBUS FIRST set foot on Cuba half a millennium ago, the island had already been attracting settlers for a long time. Indians certainly had been living there for countless generations, and new waves of immigrant tribes had been arriving for many years. Following the start of the Spanish colonization in the early Sixteenth Century, Cuba's charms began to exercise a powerful attraction on all those who knew it, friend and foe alike. In spite of its relatively small size, the island eventually became one of the most important components of the vast Spanish Empire, and Cuba came to be known as "the key to the New World."

The group of islands that lie directly south of the Bahamas in the western-most part of the Atlantic Ocean is known as the Antilles. Their collective name derives from a mythical island called *Antilia* which periodically appeared in fanciful maps drawn in Europe before the discovery of the New World.

The Antilles extend in a northwestern direction from the northern coast of South America, increasing in size as they approach the southern tip of Florida.[1] Cuba, the largest of these islands, lies at the entrance to the Gulf of Mexico, some 150 kilometers from both Florida and Yucatan. This strategic location, directly on the major sea routes to Mexico and the Caribbean ports, has played a significant role in Cuba's economic and cultural development.

The island is surrounded by some 1,600 smaller islets which together comprise a total area of 114,524 square kilometers, or a little more than half the size of Great Britain. Cuba measures some 1,900 kilometers in length[2] from its eastern tip, the Punta de Maisí, to its westernmost point, the Cabo de

A view of the Valley of San Luis near Trinidad on the south coast of Cuba. The first Spanish settlers would have encountered similar scenes as they began to explore the island. Early chronicles contain frequent references to the beauty of the Cuban landscape.

---

1   The Antilles are divided into two groups according to size: the Greater Antilles, which include Cuba, Hispaniola, Puerto Rico and Jamaica, and the Lesser Antilles, which include all the other islands from the Virgin Islands south.

2   This is approximately the distance between Chicago and Miami, or between Berlin and Madrid.

San Antonio. The island is long and narrow in shape, measuring just 57 kilometers at its narrowest point and 320 kilometers at its widest.

The Cuban landscape is a combination of gentle mountains and wide open valleys. The highest mountain range is the Sierra Maestra in Oriente, the easternmost province, where peaks rise to a maximum height of almost 2,000 meters. The fertile valleys are drained by more than 200 rivers, a feature that has greatly facilitated agricultural development. Cuba's location directly to the south of the Tropic of Cancer is the cause of its mild tropical climate. Its slender tapering shape places the entire island within reach of the soft trade winds that blow from the sea. Temperatures remain relatively uniform throughout the year, and only two seasons are known: dry and rainy.

Before the arrival of Spanish settlers, the land was covered with vast forests that included numerous fruit-bearing specimens as well as many trees yielding precious woods. Cuban cedar, ebony, and mahogany were exported to Europe for centuries, and Cuban lumber was eagerly sought in England and France as well as in Spain. Some of the very finest furniture makers in Eighteenth-Century Europe used precious Cuban woods. The quality of the mahogany once found in Cuba has never been surpassed.[3]

Cuba is blessed with an abundant fauna curiously consisting of a great variety of birds but very few indigenous mammals. Among the latter is the manatee, a heavy aquatic animal that grows up to five meters in length and is somewhat similar to a large seal. Spaniards thought manatees were mermaids when they first saw them in the water. Not without a touch of disappointment, Columbus noted that the creatures were certainly not as beautiful as mermaids were reputed to be.

Cuba's lengthy coastline is home to literally thousands of fishes and mollusks. Numerous types of colorful land snails as well as freshwater turtles can be found inland. The largest native land animals are the iguana and the *jutía*, called an "indian rat" by Columbus, which is a harmless tree rodent of up to 60 centimeters in length. There are no large cats and no poisonous snakes.

The native inhabitants of Cuba belonged to a group of Indians collectively named *Arahuacos*, or Arawaks, by the Spaniards.[4] The most primitive of these,

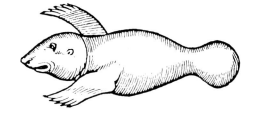

A Sixteenth-Century woodcut representing the West Indian manatee. The Spaniards encountered many new species of both plants and animals in the New World.

---

3 Sources of Cuban mahogany, which were once plentiful, have been decimated by injudicious cutting. A program of reforestation has been started, but mahogany trees need a long time to reach maturity.

4 Columbus found Arawak Indians living in all the Greater Antilles. Pockets of them also lived in the northern part of South America. Although racially identical to the other Indians who lived farther south, the Arawaks were set apart by their distinct language.

and the first to have arrived on the island, are known as the Ciboneyes, a name first recorded by Bartolomé de Las Casas in the Sixteenth Century.[5] It is likely that at one time Ciboney settlements occupied most of the island in undisturbed peace. They wore no clothes, but covered their naked bodies with painted decoration. They made a few rudimentary tools using wood or seashells. Since nature abundantly provided them with all their needs, the Ciboneyes never learned to cultivate the land.

At the time of Columbus' arrival, however, the Ciboneyes no longer dominated the island as they once had. Approximately a century earlier, a wave of more highly developed Arawak Indians appeared in eastern Cuba, proceeding most probably from Hispaniola. These new settlers, known as Tainos, eventually subjugated the Ciboneyes and forced them to move into the western part of the island, where the conquistadores were to discover only a small number of Ciboney communities.

Taino tribes had once contentedly occupied the Lesser Antilles, but they had been forced to migrate westward by the gradual spread of another group of natives, who were known as Caribs and who were as warlike and bloodthirsty as the Tainos were gentle and peaceful. For many years, Caribs had been systematically and ferociously raiding Taino settlements in the Lesser Antilles. The Caribs' practice was to kill all of the adult men, whose flesh they would then consume.[6] Young men were spared, but castrated before being taken away as slaves along with the women. It was probably around the end of the Fourteenth Century, when Carib raids were starting to threaten their settlements in Hispaniola, that the Tainos moved into Cuba. By the end of the Fifteenth Century, Tainos made up the vast majority of the island's population.

Although they never attained a high degree of cultural development, the Tainos were a great deal more advanced than their predecessors, the Ciboneyes, whom they used as slaves. Early chronicles describe them as being well-proportioned and of medium height. Their most distinctive physical charac-

5 The term Ciboney (also spelled Siboney) was originally applied by the Spaniards to the entire native population of Cuba. It is an Arawak word meaning "men of the rocks," and was derived from their practice of living in rocky caves. It was, in fact, a pejorative designation that probably came into being after the Ciboneyes were displaced by later and more sophisticated Indian settlers.

6 Columbus heard about the dreaded Caribs from various sources. Their name was variously transcribed as *Canibes*, *Canibas* or *Caribes*. In this last form the name has entered all European languages. However, it was from another variant of this spelling that the word "cannibal" was derived to denote a person who eats human flesh. The Caribbean Sea, which they dominated, was likewise named after them.

teristic was their broad foreheads. It is now known that this feature was not hereditary, but that it was deliberately induced by applying pressure on the skulls of newly-born Taino infants.

Most of what is known about Taino society is based on the chronicles of Gonzalo Fernández de Oviedo.[7] Because Oviedo spent most of his time in the New World in Hispaniola, his writings are not always reliable in trying to form a picture of life among the Cuban natives. Taino culture in Hispaniola reached a much higher degree of development, principally because of the constant threat of Carib raids, which eventually compelled the Indians to organize large federations under the control of one common authority.

This was not the case in Cuba, where the Tainos lived in small independent settlements totally isolated from each other. There were no roads through the impenetrable forests, and the rivers, or the sea, were the only ways of reaching neighboring communities. Not surprisingly, Cuban Tainos usually built their settlements on high ground near running streams. They made wooden canoes[8] which they expertly propelled with paddles. Columbus reported that an Indian canoe could move faster than a Spanish rowboat.

Taino houses, called *bohíos*, were said by Columbus to be built like Moorish tents, by which he meant they were round and had conical roofs. In fact, Taino

12

---

7 Gonzalo Fernández de Oviedo (1478–1557) was a Spanish chronicler who travelled to Hispaniola and eventually became mayor of Santo Domingo. His monumental *Historia General y Natural de las Indias* takes up no less than 30 volumes.

8 The English word canoe is derived from the Arawak *canoa*. The Tainos were extraordinarily ingenious in their method of making them. A large tree trunk would be carved out, and, after filling it with rocks, boiling water would be poured in. The combined effect of the rocks and the hot water was to expand the sides of the trunk beyond its original size.

Right: these two bohíos in the Valley of Viñales are very similar to the simple dwellings used by the Taino Indians in Cuba. Because they were unable to work stone, the Indians used only vegetable materials in the construction of their houses.

Left: the bohío has remained a common feature in Cuban rural areas. The covered porch on this modern example is a contemporary detail.

houses were either round or rectangular in shape.[9] The roof was made of palm leaves and held up by a series of supports driven into the ground around a higher central post. Walls were constructed of canes arranged very close to each other and held together by reeds.

These houses were provided with a floor of packed sand and equipped with sparse but useful furnishings. The Tainos had low wooden seats called *dujos* and slept in *hamacas*[10] which they tied inside their houses between the central post and one of the outside supports.[11] The fact that there were no doors to secure the entrance to their houses would seem to indicate that the Tainos had a highly developed sense of private property and a genuine respect for their neighbors and their possessions.

Each Taino settlement was governed by its own *cacique* whose authority was unquestioned. He regulated communal activities, such as fishing and agriculture, settled any disputes, and arranged public ceremonies. Taino dwellings were built in an irregular pattern around a large open space in front of the *cacique*'s house. This area was called the *batey* and was used for their meetings and festivities, which were usually held at night and included singing and dancing.

Several early chronicles describe the existence of a much larger *bohío* in some Taino settlements. Columbus himself reported visiting one such structure in the eastern part of Cuba, and described it as being sizable enough to house as many as 500 people. From the numerous large shells and other objects that he observed hanging from the rafters, Columbus assumed that the building was used as a temple, but the natives reportedly assured him that it was not. It seems more likely that these larger structures were intended either as communal warehouses or as public meeting rooms.

The Tainos' religious beliefs revolved around a Supreme Being who was thought to reside in the sky, but who did not figure at all in their daily lives. It

9 The rectangular *bohío* has remained the Cuban farmer's favorite dwelling. It is still a common feature of the island's landscape.

10 The Taino word *hamaca*, which was taken up unchanged into Spanish, has become "hammock" in English. It describes a loosely woven hanging cot suspended from two posts. It was easily set up, extremely cool, and kept crawling insects away. The Europeans were quick to recognize it as the ideal bed in a tropical climate, and adopted it for their own use. The Tainos had a second kind of bed, which was held up by four short posts, called a *barbacoa*. A similar contrivance was used by Mexican Indians to cook their meals, and it is that meaning that has been retained in the English word "barbecue."

11 The use of hammocks makes it possible to estimate the size of the average Taino dwelling, as the distance from the central post to the outside walls could not have exceeded two and a half meters.

was not to this deity that the Tainos prayed for protection, but to numerous natural and ancestral spirits. Finely crafted images of these benevolent beings were worn around the neck or on the forehead. Larger figures were kept in the *cacique's* house.

Taino men went around naked. The women wore skimpy cotton aprons that covered them in front from the waist to the knees. With this exception, Taino men and women appear to have enjoyed equal status in their society. Both sexes were extravagantly fond of ornamenting their bodies, wearing a great abundance of jewelry crafted out of shiny stones, feathers and shells, and painting their skin in bright colors, mostly black and red. Columbus and his men thought that the Indians' body paint was a method of keeping mosquitoes away, which certainly must have been one of the Spaniards' own perpetual concerns.

The Tainos were fairly skillful potters. Many examples of their work have been preserved, mostly utilitarian pieces meant for their daily use and decorated with geometrical patterns incised into the clay. They also made small figurines of both animal and human forms, male as well as female, which represented the spirits considered sacred by each individual community. They were equally adept at working wood, but fewer examples of their wooden utensils have survived the passage of time.

Many other objects were created by the Tainos out of various other natural materials. Their well-proportioned and finely polished axes attest to their artistic skills, as do the remarkable discs that they carefully crafted out of seashells to place in the mouth of their idols. These discs were carved on one side to simulate teeth, without which no figure was considered complete.

They cultivated cotton and used it to weave cloth and spin yarn with which they made their fishing nets and hammocks. They were excellent fishermen and cultivated various kinds of peppers to season their catch. Other agricultural products included sweet potatoes and other tubers, a great variety of fruits, and two crops which were to have a notable impact on the rest of the world: corn and tobacco.

Corn was the Tainos' principal crop.[12] Columbus observed large corn fields near the northern coast of Cuba, and collected samples to bring back to Spain. He related his discovery in a letter that he wrote to the Spanish monarchs in

---

12 The Arawak word for corn, *mahis,* has been taken up in various forms into most European languages, including English. Although "corn" is used in the United States and Canada, in England "maize" is still preferred.

November 1492. His description of the plant and its grain was the first report of corn's existence ever to reach Europe.

The Indians that Columbus and his men encountered in Cuba were a simple and happy people living in a peaceful and gentle world. They had no enemies, human or otherwise, and were therefore unused to combat. Their pathetic inability to resist the Spanish invaders made their eventual submission in the hands of the conquistadores an inevitability.

CHAPTER TWO

The Discovery

Although several descriptions of Columbus' appearance have been recorded, the numerous existing portraits of the great navigator were all done after his death. This woodcut dates from the end of the Sixteenth Century and is based on an earlier work by Paolo Giovio, a Florentine artist.

THE NIGHT WAS warm and damp on the open sea. Even in October, the sailors would have remained on deck to tell their stories and enjoy the stars. Not one of them, however, was looking into the sky that night. All eyes were focused on the horizon, for a reward of 10,000 maravedís[1] a year had been promised by the King and Queen of Spain to the first man to sight land. Two hours into the new day, on Friday the 12th of October, 1492, a lowly sailor named Rodrigo de Triana became the first Spaniard to set eyes on the New World.

Rodrigo belonged to the crew of the *Pinta*, a caravel[2] sailing under the flag of Their Most Catholic Majesties, King Ferdinand and Queen Isabella, Sovereigns of a recently united Spain. The Pinta and her two companion vessels, the *Niña* and the *Santa María*, were manned by a group of mostly Spanish sailors and renegades who had been dragooned into one of the wildest and most dangerous missions ever attempted. Some of the men had agreed to join only after they had been promised a reprieve of their death sentences.

They were simple, mostly illiterate, and highly superstitious men. They thought that the earth was flat, and supposed that any sailor who ventured too far into the vast uncharted waters of the ocean would fall off the edge of the world into an endless abyss. That they even agreed to sail at all is evidence of the persuasive powers of their captain, Christopher Columbus, who was one of the most remarkable as well as one of the strangest men of his time.

Very little is known about his early life. He was born in 1451, but the place of his birth has never been definitely established. Although it is usually believed

17

---

1 A maravedí was a copper coin in common circulation in Spain in the Fifteenth Century. It was worth one thirtieth of a real. A seaman at the time would have earned wages of beween 600 and 1,000 maravedís a month.

2 Caravel was the name given to a type of small and light ship built for speed and widely used by the Spanish and Portuguese. Both the *Pinta* and the *Niña* were caravels.

that he was born in Genoa, on the Ligurian coast of Italy, Columbus himself never claimed to be Genoese. All of his surviving writings are in Spanish, and he is not known ever to have used Italian, even when dealing with Italians, or indeed with his own family.

Columbus' bastard son, Fernando, published a biography of his father in 1541, long after the great man had died. It is a highly unreliable document, as Fernando was eager to glamorize his father's simple background. The truth seems to be that Columbus' father was a weaver, the craft also practiced by both of his grandfathers. He had three younger brothers and one younger sister, but in his later life kept in touch with only one of them, Bartolomé, who was his junior by a few years.

Columbus was a tall man with clear blue eyes and a fair, freckled complexion that would turn bright scarlet when he became angry or excited. His hair had been red in his youth, but it turned white when he was only in his thirties. Although he was a man of clear intelligence, he never received much formal education. He was single-minded and stubborn, qualities which would serve him in good stead throughout his life. He was wildly ambitious and desperately hungered for wealth and personal glory, but had to struggle for many years before attaining his goals. He was quick to take offense, unwilling to give credit to others, and unable to delegate authority, even to his closest associates.

Columbus must have been very young when he left home and took to the sea. In 1476, at the age of 25, he was shipwrecked off the coast of Portugal and, using a salvaged oar, managed to reach the shore. He made his way to Lisbon, which at that time was the meeting point of navigators and explorers from all over Europe. It was in Lisbon that he caught up with Bartolomé, his younger brother, who had also left home and taken to the sea. Bartolomé had become an expert chart maker, and some ten years later would form part of the first Portuguese expedition to sail around the Cape of Good Hope. The two brothers must have spent many happy hours discussing the extraordinary discoveries made by Portuguese navigators and dreaming about their own future.

In 1480, two years after marrying the daughter of a Portuguese seafarer, Columbus moved to Porto Santo, one of the Madeira Islands. Although located some 800 kilometres off the African coast, these islands had been colonized by Portugal, and in the Fifteenth Century they were populated by a mixture of explorers, sailors and adventurers. The stories that these men would tell of undiscovered islands lying far to the west must have set Columbus' imagination afire.

During his years in Porto Santo, Columbus earned a modest living by making maps, a trade which Bartolomé surely helped him master. As a result of his work, he spent much of his time at sea, and in time became a really expert seaman and navigator. However, his mind was set on higher goals. The excitement of discovery was in the air in Fifteenth-Century Portugal, and anyone capable of navigating a ship must have dreamed of acquiring fame and fortune in some undiscovered corner of the world.

The idea that the earth was round was not new. In the Second Century of our era, Ptolemy, the celebrated Greco-Egyptian cosmographer, had already formulated the theory. Columbus was but one of many men in Europe who believed that it was possible to reach the East by sailing westward. It was not the originality of his thinking that has earned Columbus his place in history, but rather his perseverance in the face of repeated disappointments.

History is made up of a long chain of coincidences and nothing demonstrates this better than the events that led to Columbus' discoveries. A Fifteenth-Century Florentine physician and cosmographer, Paolo dal Pozzo Toscanelli, was among those who believed that the earth was round. Toscanelli became friendly with a Portuguese canon living in Florence named Fernando Martínez de Roriz. The two men had many interests in common, and enjoyed discussing subjects such as the true shape and size of the earth.

Martínez de Roriz eventually returned to Portugal and became the confessor and adviser of King Alfonso V, a frustrated ruler who had unsuccessfully attempted to extend Portuguese domination into both Spain and North Africa. After telling the king about Toscanelli's ideas of a western sea route to the Indies, Martínez de Roriz wrote to his friend to ask for details. Toscanelli sent back a long reply, and included a map of what he believed were the seas between Europe and Asia.

Toscanelli's description of the treasures of the East were based entirely on Marco Polo's accounts of his visit to China. The riches there were beyond belief: not only gold, silver, and precious gems in great abundance, but also the spices that were so highly prized by Fifteenth-Century Europeans.[3] These remote lands were ruled by the Great Khan, who resided in Cathay. Nearby was the island of Cipango, a reference to Japan, which no European had yet visited, but whose riches were nevertheless described with similar eloquence.

3 In the Fifteenth Century, fresh provisions, particularly meat, would spoil very rapidly. Spices were used not only to add flavor, but also to mask the unpleasant taste of rotting foodstuffs. Moreover, certain spices, such as pepper, were thought to have medicinal properties.

The prospect of such fabulous gains would seem enough to have persuaded the king to undertake a voyage westward, but his advisers thought otherwise. Regardless of all the possible rewards, the risks of venturing across an immense uncharted ocean remained too daunting.

Toscanelli's map and his long letter to the king soon became well known among the eager crowd of aspiring discoverers in Lisbon. Columbus was certainly acquainted with the theories of the aging Florentine, and, in fact, actually corresponded with him. It must have been around 1482, the year Toscanelli died, that Columbus finally formulated his own plan to sail westward to the Indies. He would have to wait ten long years before reaching his goal.

King Alfonso V was succeeded by his son, John II, who is known in Portuguese history as John the Perfect. It is a memorable sobriquet for a model Renaissance ruler: a prince who was both politically astute and a patron of the arts. John was eager to find a sea route to the Indies. Under his patronage, Portuguese seafarers explored the coast of Africa, discovered the Congo, and sailed around the Cape of Good Hope. To Columbus, John II must have seemed the ideal patron. In 1483 or 1484, he managed to see the king.

Columbus was a distrustful man, and because he was only allowed to address the king in front of the entire court, he was afraid that others would listen to his ideas, appropriate them, and steal the rewards that he felt should be rightfully his. His presentation to the king seemed secretive and incoherent, and his arguments were found impossibly vague. The king judged him an impractical dreamer and dismissed him.

This map of the Greater Antilles is the work of Gerardus Mercator, the noted Flemish cartographer.

He had been living on borrowed money, and he realized that, without the king's support, he would never be able to pay it back. He had no choice but to leave Portugal in a hurry, before his creditors had him thrown in jail. It is not known exactly when or how he left, but he was in Spain by 1484.

Columbus initially sought support from powerful noblemen and not from the Crown. The Count (later Duke) of Medinaceli took him seriously enough to offer him lodging for two years, but finally decided that the scheme was too important and probably too costly for even a powerful courtier to undertake. Medinaceli sent him on to see the king and queen.

In Fifteenth-Century Spain, the court did not have a fixed location. The business of government was conducted wherever the king and queen happened to be. Ferdinand and Isabella were in Córdoba when they received Columbus in 1486. Having learned from his Portuguese experience, he must have presented a more coherent case. His proposal was referred to a group of

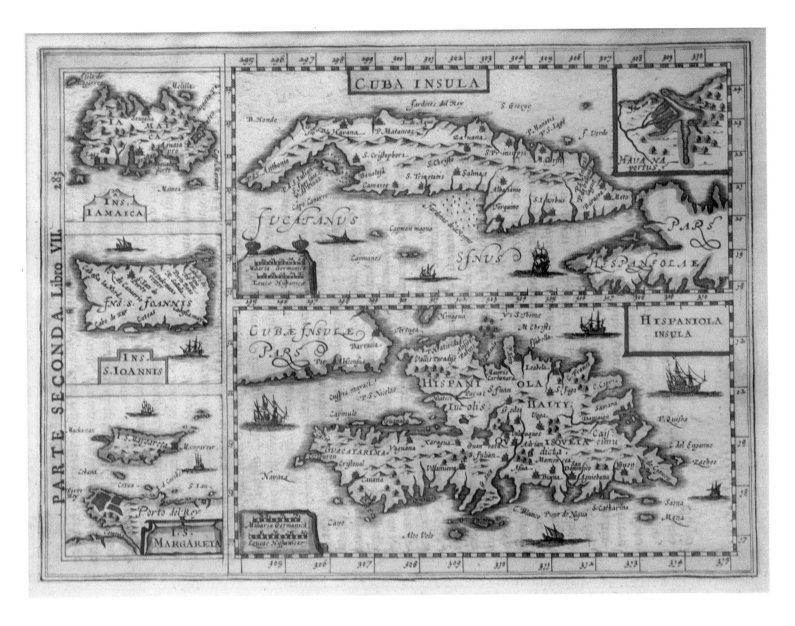

advisers, and Columbus was forced to spend the next four years following the court around Spain, pleading and hoping for a positive ruling.

By bringing together the two kingdoms of Aragon and Castile, Ferdinand and Isabella had united almost all of Spain under one crown. The two exceptions were Navarre, which was French, and Granada, the last Moorish kingdom to remain on Spanish soil. Since the Eighth Century, when the Moors had first invaded Spain, it had been the dream of every Spanish monarch to expel these intruders from their land.

By the time Ferdinand and Isabella assumed the throne, Christian and Muslim armies had been engaged in a furious war for 700 years. The conquest of Granada became the monarchs' foremost and most demanding political objective, but it proved to be a wearisome and expensive one to realize. An entire city, christened Santa Fe in honour of the Holy Faith, was built on the plain below Granada to house the multitude of Spanish soldiers.

Columbus' proposals had to compete with these pressing developments for the attention of the king and queen, but he had considerable powers of persuasion. In 1489, Columbus was granted the unusual privilege of being lodged and fed at the monarchs' expense. It was around the same time that he started living with Beatriz Enríquez, a Spanish woman who would become the mother of his son Fernando.

Throughout 1489, in spite of a massive concentration of armed forces around Granada, all the battles that were fought proved indecisive. Ferdinand and Isabella must have felt that it was wiser to defer all important matters until the Moors had been defeated. In 1490, four years after Columbus had first presented his case at court, the royal commission advised the king and queen against supporting the proposed voyage to the Indies. Although he was assured that his case had not been closed, Columbus felt defeated, and he went off to the monastery of La Rábida, in the southwestern tip of Spain. It was there that fate intervened again in the person of a mariner called Martín Alonso Pinzón.

We can only speculate what would have happened to Columbus if he had picked another spot for his retreat. Had he chosen simply to return to Portugal, or had gone anywhere else in Spain, it is unlikely that his meeting with Pinzón would ever have taken place. Without the support and encouragement that he was to receive from Pinzón and his family, it is certain that Columbus' life, and the history of the Western World, would not have been the same.

Martín Alonso Pinzón was the eldest of three brothers who were prominent shipowners and navigators in Palos de la Frontera, a small port located just a few kilometers away from La Rábida on the Atlantic coast. He was probably invited to the monastery by the prior, Juan Pérez, and immediately struck up a friendship with Columbus, who was his junior by about ten years. The two men had much in common, and the downcast Columbus must have been delighted to have found a sympathetic and influential companion with whom to share his ideas.

Pinzón mentioned to Columbus that a year earlier, while on a visit to Rome, a geographer working for Pope Innocent VIII had spoken to him about "lands that were still undiscovered." It is possible that Pinzón made up the story simply to encourage his younger friend. What is certain is that Columbus' spirits were soon restored, and that he and Pinzón became partners.

Juan Pérez, the prior who had introduced the two men, was himself an influential man with good connections in high places. He was so impressed with Columbus' project that he felt compelled to intercede for him at court. The prior must have been extremely convincing, for Queen Isabella not only invited Columbus to join her immediately in Santa Fe, but even sent him money to buy some decent clothes and a new horse.

Columbus arrived at Santa Fe just as the Spanish and Moorish armies were engaged in their final encounters, and was present at court when Boabdil, the last King of Granada, finally surrendered to Ferdinand and Isabella. At the very beginning of the new year, on the second of January 1492, the last remnant of Spanish soil still being held in infidel hands became part of Christian Spain.

It is at this stage that Columbus' life acquires an epic dimension. Seven hundred years of spiritual and political warfare had finally come to an end, and Columbus' own idealistic quest, impractical and dangerous though it must have seemed to most people at that time, nevertheless started to be seen as an extension of that holy war. The whole of Spain, convinced at last of having followed a divine cause, became intoxicated with victory. It was the perfect moment for Columbus to gain the support he had sought for so long.

Ferdinand and Isabella wanted to know what he expected as his reward. He must have had his answer ready years before anyone had asked him the question. To start with, he wanted to be ennobled, to be known as Don Cristóbal Colón.[4] He wished to be made Grand Admiral of the Ocean and Viceroy of any lands he might discover, and finally demanded one tenth of all the riches ever found there.

Not surprisingly, Columbus was turned down and dismissed once again, but not for long this time. Before he had gone very far, a horseman brought him the good news that he should return to Santa Fe. On April 17, 1492, a formal agreement with Columbus was signed by the king and queen. It granted him everything that he had requested.

He left for Palos de la Frontera, where Pinzón had already started to organize their expedition. Of the three ships that had been hired for his use, two were caravels, light in construction and around fifteen metres (50 feet) in length. However, Columbus' own flagship, the *Santa María*, was much longer and more heavily built. He would have preferred a caravel, which was much faster,

---

4 Although Columbus had been called Colom in Portugal, he started to use the Spanish form Cristóbal Colón almost immediately after his arrival in Spain, and continued to do so until his death more than twenty years later.

but a third one was not available. Although the citizens of Palos and all the other villages along the coast of Andalucía had been commanded by the Crown to place their men and provisions at Columbus' disposal, it took all of ten weeks to get the fleet ready.

It is estimated that the Crown supplied Columbus with more than one million maravedís, but still he had to borrow almost half a million more from Pinzón to cover his expenses. In addition to an immense quantity of provisions, each of the three ships carried two types of cannon in case the natives proved unfriendly. A variety of cheap trinkets was brought along to barter for gold. The most popular of these turned out to be small brass falconers' bells, which were spherical in shape and quite similar to the modern sleigh bells used today in Christmas decorations.

The expedition comprised a total of approximately 90 men, which included the owners of the three ships as well coopers, carpenters and surgeons. One of the men, Luis de Torres, who spoke Hebrew, Arabic and Chaldean, was brought along as interpreter in the event that Columbus was granted an audience by the Great Khan. As was the practice in Fifteenth-Century Europe, the crew was not provided with sleeping accomodations.

They sailed from the small port of Palos half an hour before sunrise on Friday the third of August, 1492. The captain of the *Pinta* was Martín Alonso Pinzón, with his brother Francisco serving as pilot. Another Pinzón brother, Vicente, was the captain of the *Niña*. Vicente went on to become a noted navigator in his own right and was the discoverer of the Amazon River in 1500. Columbus himself was the captain of the *Santa María*.

It immediately became clear that, as Columbus had suspected, the *Santa María* was the slowest of the three ships. But it was the *Pinta* that was to cause the most trouble. On the fourth day out, her rudder broke out of its socket. It was rumored that Cristóbal Quintero, her owner, wanted to turn back and had deliberately caused the damage. The rudder was repaired temporarily and the fleet headed for the Canary Islands to find a replacement.

Almost a month was wasted in the Canary Islands looking for another ship. Columbus finally decided simply to repair the *Pinta*. After the work was carried out to his satisfaction, and fresh provisions had been loaded, the fleet was once again ready to sail. They left on the eighth of September. A week later, long after they had lost sight of land, they watched a bright meteor fall into the sea, which the superstitious crew interpreted as a bad omen. They had been away for six weeks and had not gone very far.

This map of the New World was created by the Dutch cartographer Nicolaas Visscher in 1652. An imaginary view of Havana and its harbor can be seen in the extreme left of the upper border. Santiago de Cuba is represented at the bottom on the extreme right.

Neither Columbus nor anyone else in Europe even suspected the existence of an entirely new continent lying between Europe and Asia. Columbus planned to cross an open sea from Spain to the Indies, and had computed the distance at approximately 6,000 kilometers, or slightly less than 4,000 miles. As he was terribly secretive about his work, it is not known how he arrived at that vastly inaccurate figure. However, wrong as his calculations turned out to be, they proved extremely useful to him in his voyage west. By yet another amazing coincidence, Columbus' figures happened to be extraordinarily close to the distance between the Canary Islands and the West Indies, which was the trip that he actually made.

Columbus kept a journal during his voyage which is known to us only through a duplicate made years later by a Spanish priest called Bartolomé de Las Casas.[5] Through its daily entries, it is possible to follow Columbus' progress across the Atlantic. On the 16th of September the fleet sailed into the Sargasso Sea. The abundance of seaweed floating on the surface of the ocean was optimistically seen as evidence that they were near an island. Although he knew by his own calculations that they were still quite far from their destination, Columbus consistently interpreted this and almost all other events as proof of their proximity to land. When birds flew over the ships, and even when a whale was sighted, these were seen as signs that land had to be near, as these animals were known never to venture too far from shore.

Columbus understandably kept trying to boost the crew's spirits. No ship had ever gone so far and so long without sighting land, and the men were growing restless and unruly. When recording the distance traveled each day, he always subtracted a few leagues to make sure that the men would not realize just how far from home they actually were and become even more alarmed. It was reported to him, and he noted it in his journal on the 24th of September, that the crew had proposed tossing him into the sea and sailing home with the story that their captain had met with an unfortunate accident.

Columbus needed all of his extraordinary powers of persuasion to overcome these crises. He was fighting raw superstitious fear with assurances that he himself must have been beginning to misdoubt. It was his turn to seek encouragement, and fortunately Martín Pinzón was at hand. The very next day, on the evening of the 25th of September, Pinzón reported that he had sighted land to the southwest. The men were delirious and, with their faith restored, climbed up the masts shouting that they, too, could see land. After saying a prayer of thanksgiving, Columbus ordered the fleet to follow a southwesterly course. The next morning, however, whatever it was that had been sighted had disappeared.

They sailed all of the next day and night without seeing anything, and for the following four days there was no wind at all, which slowed the ships down. These were the most difficult days of the voyage. The men's disappointment was turning into anger, and the specter of mutiny was in the air. There was heavy rain on the first of October, and the wind picked up after that. On Satur-

5 Bartolomé de Las Casas (1474–1566) was a Spanish priest and historian who traveled to the New World in 1502 and became the great protector of the native Indians. He wrote a comprehensive and highly detailed *Historia de las Indias*.

day the sixth, Martín Pinzón suggested following a southwesterly course once again, but Columbus refused.

Each of the three ships kept trying to sail in front of the others in order to increase their chance of being the first to sight land and thereby collect the reward that had been offered by the king and queen. On the seventh of October, the crew of the *Niña*, which had sailed ahead, reported sighting land, but it turned out to be another mirage. Because there had been so many of these bogus sightings, Columbus decreed that any man responsible for a false report would be ineligible to collect any possible reward.

A large flock of birds was observed flying to the southwest, and this finally convinced the admiral to follow Pinzón's advice. The fleet changed course on the eighth of October, and all throughout the following night, birds could be heard flying overhead. They covered a great distance the next day, but failed to sight land, which made the crew restless and unhappy again. On the eleventh, in a rough sea, clear evidence that they were near land washed up to the ships. The men picked up reeds, a branch with flowers and even a carved stick. Land was finally sighted that night from a distance estimated by Columbus at two leagues. It was ten weeks to the day since they had left the port of Palos.

They had arrived on a small island located almost in the center of the Bahamian archipelago. Known to the natives as Guanahani, it was baptised San Salvador by Columbus in honour of the Holy Saviour, and was later called Watling Island by the English. Shortly after dawn on the morning of the 12th of October, Columbus came ashore with his two fellow captains and the other officials of his fleet. They carried the royal standard, which they planted on the shore, and claimed the island in the name of the King and Queen of Spain. Although Columbus does not mention it in his journal, the crew probably came along to celebrate, as it would have been very difficult, and in fact foolhardy, to leave them alone on the ships.

The Spaniards spent some ten days quietly sailing around Guanahani. Columbus was convinced that he and his men had indeed arrived in the Indies as he had planned, and therefore the natives they encountered were called Indians by him in his journal. Curiously, it is one of the very few of Columbus' appellations to have survived unchanged.

How the Spaniards communicated with the Indians remains a mystery, but somehow they managed to learn that the gold that they used for their small ornaments came from a larger island to the south called Colba or Cuba.[6] Columbus assumed that this referred to Cipango, the fabled island kingdom described by Marco Polo, and decided to sail there without delay. He stopped at every little island on his way south, giving each a name and a cross before moving on. It was on the evening of the 27th of October that Cuba was sighted at last. A range of mountains could be made out clearly beyond the horizon, and the Spaniards fired shots into the air to celebrate their newest and most important discovery.

They waited until the next morning to investigate further. The ships had anchored directly in front of a bay, and small boats were sent out to check the depth of the water. The bay turned out to be the wide estuary of a river, and more than deep enough for the ships.[7] Columbus went ashore and took possession of the island for Ferdinand and Isabella, naming it Juana in honour of their son and heir, Don Juan. Columbus described it as the fairest land that human eyes had ever seen.

28

6 Neither the natives found by Columbus in Cuba nor those he encountered in any of the other Antillian islands had ever developed a written language. The Spaniards made an effort to write down what names and sounds they could make out, but spelling was an inexact discipline in Fifteenth-Century Europe. Indian words were almost always written down in a variety of different ways.

7 Columbus named this estuary "Puerto de Mares." It has proved impossible to ascertain its precise location. However, it is likely that Columbus' first arrival in Cuba took place in one of the several large bays found on the northern coast of the province of Oriente.

CHAPTER THREE

Diego Velázquez and the Colonization

THE SPANIARDS' PARAMOUNT objective in America was to procure large quantities of gold. Marco Polo's description of the fabulous riches of the Indies was the fuel that had kept Columbus and his men going on their perilous adventure. They were immediately drawn to the small gold ornaments worn by the Indians, and traded them for the cheap trinkets they had brought from Spain.

When Columbus first arrived in Cuba, he hoped that he had found the source of the Indians' gold. Unfortunately, that precious metal is not among Cuba's otherwise plentiful natural resources. Gold is found on the island only in very small quantities. The Spaniards were disappointed and moved on. Hispaniola was to become their initial base of operations in the New World.

It was not until 1508 that Spanish eyes turned once again to Cuba. The governor of Hispaniola assigned one of the men under his command, Sebastián de Ocampo, to explore the Cuban coastline, a project that the Crown had wanted to undertake for a long time and that in the end would take more than eight months to complete.[1]

Much had happened in the sixteen years since the island had been discovered. Queen Isabella had died in 1504, bequeathing the crown of Castile and Leon to her daughter, Joanna. This unfortunate woman, who has become known in history as Joanna the Mad, had lost both her husband and her reason and was unable to rule. King Ferdinand, her father, acted as regent in her place.

Columbus was promised by Ferdinand and Isabella to be made Viceroy and

---

1 Sebastián de Ocampo was a native of Galicia in the northern part of Spain and a former servant of Queen Isabella. He explored the coastline of Cuba with two caravels, starting along the northern shore and traveling in a westerly direction. Ocampo discovered, among others, the bay of Havana, which he named Carenas. He was the first to circumnavigate Cuba, and thereby established that it was an island and not part of a continent, as Columbus had believed.

governor of any lands he would discover on his voyages. However, he had fallen out with the sovereigns and ended his days in disgrace. After Columbus' death in 1506, his son Diego was forced to take legal action to secure his own rights. The King remained weary of Diego's political ambitions, and it was not until 1509 that the younger Columbus was finally allowed to take charge of Hispaniola.

By the time Diego arrived in the New World, he was eager to consolidate and expand his family's patrimony. Ocampo had just returned from Cuba with detailed reports that the island offered excellent opportunities for development. Diego wanted to send an expedition to conquer and settle Cuba, and proposed doing so under the command of his uncle Bartolomé.

Diego's plan proved controversial among the conquistadores in Hispaniola, who were divided into two factions: one that supported the rights of Columbus' family, and another that upheld King Ferdinand's ultimate authority. It was the latter group that enjoyed greater influence at court, and the projected expedition was delayed until a commander who was acceptable to both sides could be found.

Diego Columbus eventually reconsidered his position and asked Diego Velázquez to command the campaign. Velázquez had sailed to the New World in 1493 on Columbus' second voyage. He was wealthy and successful, a man accustomed to exercising power. Las Casas says that he had "a cheerful and humane disposition, and enjoyed great esteem as a result of the convivial and unassuming manner in which he treated his subordinates, without diminishing either his dignity or the respect due him and his position."

Diego Columbus could not have made a better choice. Velázquez had experience in dealing with the Indians and had already founded several settlements in Hispaniola. He also had the backing of the King's supporters. To protect himself, Diego Columbus named one of his own allies, Francisco de Morales, as second in command. Both appointments were confirmed by King Ferdinand. Many volunteers came forward to join the campaign.

Velázquez was a mature man of almost fifty when he sailed to Cuba early in 1511. He chose the shortest possible crossing from Hispaniola and landed almost at the easternmost tip of the island, near the Punta de Maisí. The first Spanish settlement in Cuba was founded nearby and given an Indian name, Baracoa. Although its port is not particularly impressive, Baracoa lies on the north coast directly next to a mountain nearly 2000 meters in height and quite distinctive in shape, and this provided the settlers with a useful natural land-

Most of Cuba was covered with thick tropical vegetation when the first Spanish colonists arrived. Water was the only possible means of transportation until roads could be constructed through the forests. The Spaniards followed the example of the Indians in building their settlements near rivers or the sea. Sancti Spíritus was founded in 1514 on the banks of the River Yayabo in the central province of Las Villas. The brick bridge was built in 1815.

mark for navigation.[2] Velázquez made Baracoa his capital and the center of his operations in Cuba.

The conquistadores' practice of subjugating the natives with unmerciful harshness had had devastating results in Hispaniola. Velázquez had spent more than eighteen years living under that system and, having found it ineffective and cruel, he determined to follow a different course in Cuba. Unfortunately, not all of his companions were in agreement with him. Francisco de Morales, whose real goal was to supplant Velázquez, was among those who did not think that the Indians should be treated with any greater moderation and kindness.

Velázquez' benevolent intentions were discarded almost from the beginning as the Indians resisted the Spaniards' advance. It must be said to Velazquez'

32

---

2   El Yunque, which is 1932 meters high, was named after its resemblance to an anvil.

Right: the first Spanish cities in Cuba were carefully planned. Land was set aside on the principal square for the construction of a church. The cathedral of Camagüey was built much later on the site of an earlier and simpler structure. The city is one of the oldest in Cuba and was originally named Santa María del Puerto del Príncipe.

Left: this memorial plaque commemmorates the accidental death of Doña María de Cepero while praying in the main church of Havana in 1557. By that time, the importance of Havana's port had been recognized by Spain's adversaries. Doña María had survived the occupation of the city by Jacques de Sores. The church where she had been saying her prayers must have suffered serious damage at the hands of the French corsair. This plaque is the oldest remaining historical monument in Cuba.

credit that he invariably attempted to curb his subordinates' worst excesses in dealing with the natives, but he could not be everywhere at once, and great injustices were committed in his name. Part of the Indian population fled to the west, unable to resist the invaders but unwilling to submit to the severity of their rule. However, some pockets of Indians continued to engage the conquistadores in pitiful skirmishes and were invariably massacred en masse.

One particular *cacique*, named Hatuey, showed great courage and determination in fighting the invaders. His efforts were useless, and he was eventually captured and executed along with his followers. As he was about to be burned at the stake, the Indian leader was offered conversion and baptism by a well-meaning Franciscan. Legend has it that Hatuey refused the good friar's offer on the grounds that he had no wish to go to Heaven since he never again wanted to see another Spaniard.

Left: Trinidad was built on the south coast of Cuba. The Caribbean Sea can be seen clearly from the hills north of the city.

Below: the house of Diego Velázquez is located on the main square of Santiago de Cuba.

It did not take Velázquez long to bring the entire eastern part of Cuba under Spanish control. King Ferdinand must have been pleased with the progress, and offered the settlers in Cuba important benefits which were essential to their continued presence on the island. In various royal decrees dated 1512 and 1513, Velázquez and his men were granted the privilege to receive regular supplies from the Crown as well as foodstuffs and cattle. They were also given the right of ownership of any buildings they constructed and of any land they held, and were empowered to organize municipalities and to appoint judges and other public officials.

Although Velázquez remained under the jurisdiction of Diego Columbus in Hispaniola, he was granted wider authority. Soon he determined to expand the territory under his control. To this end, he organized three expeditions into the west of the island. One of these was to follow the north coast of Cuba as far as the bay of Carenas, the present site of Havana. The second was to travel by land to the same destination. The third, which was led by Velázquez himself, was to follow the southern coast as far as the bay of Jagua, the present site of Cienfuegos.

Six additional settlements were started in the course of these expeditions: Bayamo, Sancti Spíritus, Trinidad, Puerto Príncipe, Havana and Santiago de Cuba. Together with Baracoa, these cities, all founded before the end of 1514, are known in Cuban history as the first seven villages. Velázquez' intention had been to situate these new settlements in different parts of the island, and it became apparent to him that Baracoa was too isolated to continue functioning as his center of operations. The capital was transferred to Santiago de Cuba, located on the banks of a magnificently spacious bay on the south shore.

These early Cuban cities were laid out in a methodical manner which represents one of the earliest examples of urban planning in the New World. After marking the boundaries of the municipality, land would be set aside for a central square, a church, a market, a school, a prison, and all other public buildings. Private individuals received land grants according to their social status. Peons or laborers were granted *peonías* of approximately 500 square meters,[3] whereas gentlemen—*caballeros* in Spanish—were granted *caballerías* of double this extension. All those receiving land grants were urged to build their own houses, but obtained full ownership rights to them only after having been in residence for four years.

Havana was initially founded on the south coast of Cuba, but the site was found to be unhealthy and the settlement was transferred to its present location in 1519. The fortress of El Morro was built by the Spanish to guard the narrow entrance channel to the bay.

3 In principle, the *peonía* consisted of 5000 square feet, but in practice these measures were not strictly enforced.

Agricultural land was parceled out in a similar manner. Peons were given approximately 6400 square meters,[4] plus grain for cultivation, one hundred sheep, twenty cows, ten sows, twenty goats and five horses. Gentlemen were granted five times these figures. Land that was not given in grant was reserved for common use and remained the property of the king.

Tools and weapons, powder, clothing, paper, and various types of religious articles all had to be brought from Spain, as were farm animals, chickens and other domesticated fowl, wine, olive oil and flour. Many Spanish plants were transported to the New World and some of these were successfully grown in Cuba. In spite of these imports, the diet of the early settlers consisted mainly of

38

4   The actual Spanish measure was 100 *fanegas* of land. The word fanega had two different meanings. It was used as a cubic measure for grain. By extension, the area needed to sow that quantity of wheat was also called a *fanega*. Sixteenth-Century units of measurement were widely imprecise.

Right: the principal church (Parroquial Mayor) in Sancti Spíritus dominates the center of the old city.

Below left: the Hospital de San Juan de Dios in Camagüey is an immense building. This view shows a side entrance to the hospital church.

Below right: although large areas of Havana had to be rebuilt in the Eighteenth Century, the original layout of the city has been preserved. This view shows one of the towers of the Cathedral.

the same staples that had sustained their Indian predecessors. In addition to the great variety of fruits native to the island, the Spanish soon learned to value corn and cassava,[5] which have remained basic ingredients of Cuban cuisine until today.

During the first quarter of the Sixteenth Century, all traffic to and from Spain passed through Santo Domingo, which was at that time the busiest and most important port in the New World. Hispaniola was then the principal Spanish colony in the Americas. It was only as a result of its greater proximity to that island that the eastern part of Cuba had been the first to be developed. Meanwhile, news of Columbus' discoveries had brought on an epidemic of

Left: the Church of San Francisco de Paula is one of the oldest in Havana.

Below: the fortress of El Morro in Santiago de Cuba overlooks the entrance to one of the largest and most important harbors on the island.

41

5 The English word cassava is derived from the Arawak *casabi*, which denoted a kind of flat bread made by the Indians from the ground and dried roots of a shrub of the genus *Manihot* and which they called *yuca*. It is this word which has been retained in Spanish.

exploration fever in Europe, and the Spanish were aware of the urgency to spread their empire before the numerous navigators who were making their way across the ocean could stake out claims of their own. Spanish expeditions to explore and settle the mainland were to change the course of Cuba's development. Eventually, Cuba's ties to Hispaniola were almost entirely severed, and, as one prospered, the other declined.

Velázquez was an ambitious man and, as it became more and more evident that Cuba would not yield gold in the quantities for which he had hoped, he started to cast a wandering eye over the surrounding territories. However, King Ferdinand did not want his governor to devote himself to anything other than the further finding and exploitation of the island's resources, and he refused Velázquez permission to set out on exploratory expeditions of his own.

This ban was lifted only after King Ferdinand's death in 1516, when the throne passed to his grandson, who became King Charles I of Spain, but who is better known in history as the Emperor Charles V. In 1517, a fleet left Cuba under the direction of one of Velázquez' men, Francisco Hernández de Córdoba, with the aim of exploring the coast of Yucatan. He met with strong resistance from the natives and lost many of his 120 men before sailing back.

The following year, a much larger expedition left for Yucatan under the direction of Velazquez' nephew, Juan de Grijalva. He explored the Mexican coast as far as Veracruz, and returned to Cuba with reports of Montezuma's rich empire. This news convinced Velázquez to devote his efforts to the conquest of Mexico. He requested the king for permission to go on with his ambitious plans, and, at the end of 1518, was authorized to proceed.

Velázquez' third Mexican expedition consisted of eleven ships carrying 700 Spanish and 1000 Indian men. They were equipped with cannons and other weapons as well as with horses and ample provisions for their journey. Velázquez never fully trusted Hernán Cortés, the man he had initially chosen as leader, and at the last minute decided to take command himself.[6] However, Cortés got wind of this news before Velázquez had time to act, and sailed from

6 Hernán Cortés was born in the Spanish city of Medellín in 1485. He studied at the University of Salamanca, but left to go to Hispaniola, where he arrived at the age of nineteen and where he settled as a farmer and notary. He accompanied Velázquez to Cuba in 1511 and served as the governor's secretary.. He later became mayor of Santiago de Cuba at the time when it was the island's capital. After his arrival in Mexico, he burned his ships to prevent any of his men from returning to Cuba. He was ruthless and cruel in his treatment of the Indians, and although he was eventually ennobled by the king, he never attained the office of governor. He died in Spain in 1547, a rejected and unhappy man.

the port of Santiago de Cuba under cover of night, disobeying his governor, but embarking on a brilliant venture that would earn him a place in history.

Velázquez was unwilling to accept either Cortés' treachery or the loss of a campaign that he had spent a great deal of time, effort and his own funds to organize. He immediately started a fourth expedition, larger and better equipped than the previous one. In 1520, more than 1000 Spaniards sailed for Veracruz on eighteen ships loaded with cannons and horses. The commander was Pánfilo de Narváez. Unfortunately, all of Velázquez' efforts ended up only helping Cortés. Narváez was captured and returned to Cuba, but most of the men under his command chose to stay behind.

Although Velázquez remained undeterred and even started to plan a fifth campaign, he was ordered by the king to cease all further efforts to interfere with the conquest of Mexico. In spite of this setback, Velázquez' achievements in Cuba were many and of lasting value. By the time of his death in 1524, he had laid the foundation of Cuba's future development as the hub of a burgeoning Spanish Empire in the New World.

CHAPTER FOUR

Padre Las Casas and the Introduction of Black Slavery

44   THE COLONIZATION OF the New World obviously entailed a considerable amount of physical effort. There was a great deal of hard work to be done, and settlers could not be sent from Spain in sufficient numbers to manage it all. Forests had to be cleared, roads had to be laid out, houses and public buildings had to be constructed, and, most importantly, fields needed to be tilled and sowed. Added to all these labors was the ongoing search for gold. Columbus certainly intended to enslave the Indians and use them as laborers. Most of the earliest settlers in Cuba shared his view that the natives should be forcibly put to work to cover the myriad needs of the growing colony.

The year that Columbus first landed in Cuba saw the election of a Spaniard, Cardinal Rodrigo Borgia, to the Papal Throne. Borgia, who took the name of Alexander VI, was asked by Ferdinand and Isabella to confirm their rights over the lands Columbus had encountered in the New World. The Pope agreed, and, in 1493, granted the Spanish monarchs sovereignty over any territories discovered or to be discovered by them or their successors, as long as these lands did not already belong to another Christian prince. At the same time, they were obliged by the Pope to Christianize the natives, who were not to be enslaved under any circumstances. In an attempt to get around the Pope's prohibition, and still secure a large supply of cheap labor, the Spanish developed the system of encomiendas.[1]

The crown would entrust a certain number of Indians, who were called *encomendados*, to a Spanish settler of good standing, who was known as the *encomendero*. In exchange for the Indians' free labor, the *encomendero* was expected to lodge, clothe and feed them in an adequate manner. More importantly, he was required to give the natives under his care instruction in the Christian Faith.

Right: Blacks and Whites have always mixed freely in Cuba. The women and children seen in this picture all share a building in the old part of Havana.

Below: African slaves were brought to Cuba in great numbers during more than 350 years. Their descendants make up a large part of the population of the island.

---

1   The Spanish word *encomendar* literally means to entrust or commit with confidence.

In principle, encomiendas were temporary. The Indians were supposed to be given their freedom as soon as they had been converted to Christianity and adequately trained. Encomiendas could be revoked if the *encomendero* ever failed in his duties or treated his dependents with undue harshness.

In practice, the *encomenderos* exercised unfettered control over their charges. Knowing that the Indians were supposed to be in their service for only a limited time, the *encomenderos* exploited them without mercy. Badly fed and overworked, thousands of unfortunate natives died in Hispaniola and Cuba during the first years of the Sixteenth Century.

During his years in Hispaniola, Velázquez had known a Spanish priest named Bartolomé de Las Casas. This extraordinary man had studied at the University of Salamanca and had come to the New World in 1502. He was ordained a Dominican priest eight years later. In 1511, shortly after his arrival in Cuba, Velázquez asked Las Casas to join him. The priest was granted land in the central region of the island as well as a suitable encomienda of Indians.

Although Las Casas had known the system of encomiendas in Hispaniola and was aware of its inherent evils, he accepted the established order during his first years in Cuba. His own *encomendados* were put to work panning for gold. However, other Dominicans on the island were actively preaching against the forced exploitation of the Indians. One of these priests supposedly denied Las Casas absolution on the grounds of his involvement in this inhuman practice.

It was not until 1514 that Las Casas decided to renounce his encomienda and dedicate his life to the abolition of the system. He relates in his memoirs that, while preparing a sermon for Pentecost Sunday that year, a passage from the Scriptures made him realize the error of his ways. From that moment on, he devoted all his efforts to publicizing the evils of the encomiendas. He became known as "The Protector of the Indians." It is largely due to him that the Spanish Crown eventually abolished the encomiendas in 1542.

By this time, Cuba's Indian population had been drastically diminished. Thousands of natives had been forcibly taken away on the various expeditions that had left for Mexico. Moreover, the Spaniards had brought many germs to the New World to which the Indians had never been exposed and against which they had not developed any kind of immunity.[2] Smallpox, added to the

---

2 Germs traveled across the ocean in both directions. Syphilis had been unknown in Europe until 1495. It is speculated that it was carried there by sailors returning from the New World.

long hours of work and their inadequate nourishment, further reduced the numbers of natives in Cuba to a few small communities in the eastern part of the island. Even before the abolition of the encomiendas, it had become clear to the Spanish Crown that a new source of cheap labor had to be found to replace the Indians.

Although the slave trade rightly appears immoral and evil to modern man, it was certainly not perceived in that manner during the Sixteenth Century. The system had been known in Europe since Biblical times, and was common in the ancient world. Slaves had been brought to Portugal from Africa as early as 1440. Even a man as compassionate and merciful as Bartolomé de Las Casas initially accepted the importation of black slaves as a perfectly legitimate practice. Africans were thought to have a stronger physical constitution than Indians, and therefore were considered able to endure the rigors of forced labor.

The first Spanish documents relating to the slave trade date from 1501. However, it is not known precisely when the first Africans arrived in the New World. By 1503, their numbers in Hispaniola had swelled to such proportions that steps were taken to limit their importation. The first reference to the practice in Cuba dates from 1513, when a Spaniard named Amador de Lares was authorized to bring four Africans with him from Hispaniola. Three hundred years later, the black population of Cuba would outnumber all other racial groups.

The slave trade eventually became a widespread and profitable enterprise in Spanish America, particularly in the area around the Caribbean Sea. From the beginning, the trade was strictly regulated. After the union of the the Spanish and Portuguese crowns under King Philip II, numerous Portuguese merchants were granted concessions to import African slaves into the New World. In 1595, a trader named Gómez Reynel was authorized to transport 4,500 Africans annually for a period of nine years. Most of these were destined for the Antilles.

Black slaves arrived in Cuba in culturally homogeneous groups. In this manner, the Spanish system differed fundamentally from its counterpart in North America. Africans in Cuba were allowed to live and work with members of their own tribes, and, therefore, were able to retain their indigenous language, religion and traditions to a remarkable degree. Cuban slaves kept their African roots alive and were able to draw from the well of their own culture. The considerable contributions made by Africans to Cuban life, which are most evident in the field of music, were made possible only by this fact.

The descendants of slaves have played an important role in Cuban life. Cuban music shows a marked African influence.

Blacks and whites mixed freely in Cuba from the earliest years of the colonization. The population of the island eventually became a mixture of Spaniards, Creoles,[3] blacks and mulattoes.[4] All children of slave women were born slaves, regardless of the father's race, unless the slave owner chose to grant them their freedom. Occasionally, a slave mother was able to buy her child's freedom before his birth. Liberated slaves usually moved to the larger Cuban cities, where they were allowed to live, work and marry without any restrictions.

Ever since the initial arrival of African slaves, settlers in Cuba had hoped that the regulations restricting their importation would be relaxed. It was only in 1789 that the free trade in slaves was finally authorized by Spain, and then only for a period of two years. During this time, more than 20,000 Africans arrived on the island.

In 1791, an insurgence of black slaves took place in Haiti, which had been a French colony. In the course of the Eighteenth Century, Haiti had become the world's primary source of sugar and other tropical products. The total collapse of its economy was seen in Cuba as a great opportunity to take over this lucrative market. An eminent Cuban economist called Francisco de Arango y Parreño made an impassioned appeal to the Spanish King Charles IV to permanently relax the trade restrictions that were holding back the development of the island.

The price of sugar had risen to more than seven times the level it had been just six years earlier. The King recognized that enormous profits were to be made in Cuba. In November 1791, the free importation of slaves was authorized, initially for a period of six years, but eventually in perpetuity. During the years immediately following this decree, unprecedented numbers of African slaves arrived in Cuba to work in the sugar industry.

In 1868, at the beginning of the struggle for independence from Spain, the Cuban landowner and patriot Carlos Manuel de Céspedes granted freedom to all his slaves. Africans and Creoles fought side by side against Spanish soldiers, united under a common cause. However, slavery would remain legal in Spain and her colonies until 1886.

3 The term Creole refers to the offspring of Spanish or other European parents, but born in the New World. A Spaniard born in Spain was known in Cuba as a *peninsular*, his Cuban children as Creoles.

4 The term mulatto refers to someone having one European and one African parent. An elaborate system of nomenclature developed in Spanish America to define almost all possible combinations among races.

The largest sugar plantations had a population of hundreds of slaves. They were summoned to their daily chores from towers like this one, built on the estate of the Iznaga family near Trinidad. Watchmen made sure that no slaves would run away.

CHAPTER FIVE

Tobacco and Sugar

Τ HE HISTORY OF Cuba has been shaped by nature. Its location would make the island the principal component of an immense network of communication and trade between Spain and her possessions in the New World. Likewise, the fertile soil of Cuba's open valleys would be the determining factor in developing the island's primarily agricultural economy. Two crops have dominated Cuban agriculture since the beginning of the colonization: tobacco and sugar.

Columbus reports in his journal that the Indians of Cuba, both men and women, walked around "with sticks in their hands, burning herbs they would inhale." The Spaniards had casually discovered a Cuban custom that would eventually take over the entire world. The tobacco plant, which is indigenous to Cuba, was widely cultivated by the Indians. They rolled the leaves into the primitive cigars described by Columbus. Tobacco was also ground into a powder and burned in curious Y-shaped pipes which the Indians placed in their nostrils to inhale the smoke. The Indians called tobacco *cohiba* and the pipe *tabaco*. However, the Spanish initially believed that one word applied to both the pipe and the weed that it contained, and it was by this mistaken appellation that the novelty became known in Europe.

The systematic cultivation of tobacco in Cuba was started by the Spanish as early as 1580 and was well established within the following 50 years. By the end of the Seventeenth Century, the tobacco trade had attained such importance in Europe that the French Crown had imposed a system to control the cultivation and marketing of the leaf. In 1700, Philip V, who had been born in France, became King of Spain. One of his ministers, Jean Orry,[1] implemented a similar scheme in Spain to the detriment of Cuban growers. The Spanish

The best tobacco leaf has always been grown in an area of the province of Pinar del Río called Vuelta Abajo. Nearby is the valley of Viñales, known for its exotic beauty.

---

1 Jean Orry (1652–1719) was a French economist who was sent to Spain by Louis XIV, Philip V's grandfather. Orry devised a plan to reorganize the Spanish financial and administrative systems, and eventually became one of the powers behind the throne. He was very unpopular in Spain.

Crown was to have a total monopoly over the production and exportation of tobacco.

From the outset, the superior quality of Cuban leaf had been appreciated by the authorities. It was decided that Cuba would be the main supplier of tobacco to Spanish factories. In 1708, a new governor, Laureano de Torres,[2] arrived in Havana with the commission to secure an annual supply of three million pounds of tobacco of the highest quality. The Royal Treasury in Mexico was commanded to supply the necessary funds.

Torres was followed by Vicente Raja. The new governor arrived in Cuba in 1716 with a committee to study the tobacco industry, which had become the island's most profitable enterprise. Tobacco leaf was light in weight and easily transportable. Its cultivation did not require a large investment of either funds or labor. Moreover, Cuban tobacco was of unsurpassed quality and in great demand. For all these reasons, the Spanish Crown, which was in ever greater need of revenue, decided to expand the cultivation of tobacco on the island, but under even greater controls. Stricter regulations were introduced in 1717 to eliminate private dealing and impose a fixed price on the output of Cuban growers, who reacted with predictable displeasure. Merchants were equally unwilling to allow the Treasury to interfere with their flourishing business.

More than 500 tobacco planters marched to Havana in August 1717 to protest against the new monopoly laws and to demand their repeal. The protesters occupied the city and managed to cut off supplies to the governor's forces. After three days of negotiations, Governor Raja was forcibly boarded onto a ship and sent back to Spain. However, the growers' victory was not to last for long. A new governor, Gregorio Guazo Calderón, was dispatched to Cuba in 1718 with firm instructions to enforce the tobacco monopoly and to suppress any further protests.

The most hated aspect of the tobacco monopoly was that the Treasury was not under any obligation to buy the entire output of the Cuban growers. On the other hand, the growers were not allowed to sell whatever part of their production had not been bought by the Treasury, no matter how large this surplus was, or how much local demand there existed for it. Because of these discriminatory regulations, the tobacco industry in Cuba continued to be plagued by trouble throughout the Eighteenth Century. Harmony would

2   Philip V granted Laureano de Torres the title of Marqués de Casa Torres in recognition of his success in Cuba.

come only after the final repeal of the tobacco monopoly in 1817, due largely to the efforts of Francisco de Arango y Parreño.

In the course of the Nineteenth Century, Cuban tobacco became universally recognized as the finest in the world, a position it still enjoys. Although the plant is cultivated throughout the island, the best leaf has always been grown in a small area called Vuelta Abajo, which is located in the easternmost province of Pinar del Río. Even today, production methods remain as they were in the past. To avoid spoiling the taste of the leaf, pesticides are never used. Instead, nets are laboriously erected over the tobacco fields to keep insects away. The unique sight of these vast constructions is typical of the Vuelta Abajo landscape.

Cuban cigars are still rolled by hand in the traditional manner using only natural products. Although not all cigars are rolled in Havana, many of the larger tobacco firms are located there, and it is as Havana cigars that they have become known everywhere. The gift of Cuba's fertile land, a Havana cigar has always been the island's most excellent ambassador to the entire world.

Sugar cane was brought to Hispaniola by Columbus in 1493, on his second voyage to the New World. [3] The plant was taken to Cuba by Velázquez in 1511, and its cultivation on the island was started without delay. In 1595, King Philip II authorized the establishment of sugar factories in Cuba. Any equipment needed for the new enterprise was exempted from import duties, and the sum of 40,000 ducats was made available from the Royal Treasury to be given as loans to those sugar planters who were willing to start production.

By 1602, seventeen sugar factories were in operation. The largest of these employed 28 slaves, and the smallest only two. The majority of the early sugar planters were Portuguese. At first, production was concentrated in the area around Havana. Eventually, sugar plantations would be found throughout the entire island.

The cultivation of sugar cane in the Antilles spread very rapidly. By the end of the Sixteenth Century, sugar production in Spanish America had attained such proportions that it is now considered to have been the largest industrial enterprise that existed in the world at that time. This new industry had a tremendous impact in the economy, eating habits and customs of the Old World.

---

3 The sugar cane plant is indigenous to New Guinea. Its cultivation was widespread in Asia from ancient times. The word sugar is derived from the Sanskrit *sarkara*, as is the Spanish word *azúcar*. Arab traders brought the plant to North Africa, and from there it spread throughout the world.

Up to then, sugar had been a great luxury sold very sparingly in pharmacies. The dramatic increase in its availability suddenly placed it within everyone's reach. All countries have certain sweet delicacies that are prepared to celebrate various religious and family holidays and that are considered a special part of national traditions. What is not always realized is that none of these, from Viennese strudels to English plum pudding, Swiss chocolates and German marzipan, could have been created without the abundant supply of sugar that started arriving in Europe from the New World.

The harvesting of the sugar cane and subsequent manufacture of sugar require intensive physical labor. For this reason, the evolution of the sugar industry in the Antilles is closely connected to the development of the slave trade. The vast majority of the African slaves that arrived in Cuba went to work in sugar plantations. In the Nineteenth Century, the largest of these had a population of many hundreds of resident slaves.

54

Most tobacco merchants had their offices in Havana. This view shows the headquarters of one of the oldest, Partagás, in the center of the city.

The sugar cane plant looks much like corn and has long fibrous stalks that reach a height of approximately two meters. The cutting and harvesting of sugar cane is a grueling process that has always been done by hand. The stalks must be taken to the mill before they dry out. They are then crushed to extract their sap. This sweet greenish juice is boiled down to produce molasses, which can either be used directly as a sweetener in cooking, or can be further boiled down to obtain raw sugar. Until the end of the Nineteenth Century, the final step of the manufacturing process was to pour the boiling liquid into molds, where it would solidify as it cooled. At that time, sugar was shipped in conical loaves weighing up to two kilograms. Chunks were broken off as needed.

Slaves were brought to Cuba in ever greater numbers after 1791, when the regulations that had limited their importation were lifted. The increase in the labor supply resulted in a boom for the sugar industry. By 1835, the average quantity of sugar annually exported from Cuba was almost 91 million kilograms. Five years later, this amount had grown by 28% to almost 117 million kilograms.[4] At one point, there were more than 1200 sugar mills operating on the island. The Spanish had found a different kind of gold in Cuba.

The profits to be made in sugar began attracting investors from other parts of Europe. By 1840, the Spanish had ceased to be the principal source of capital in the industry. Many French and German immigrants acquired plantations in the area around Trinidad, which at that time produced more than one third of the total amount of sugar exported from the island.

In the Nineteenth Century, the larger sugar establishments resembled small villages. The most ambitious building was the residence of the proprietor and his family. The one at the *Ingenio de Jesús Nazareno de Buena Vista*, in the Valley of San Luis outside Trinidad, is one of the few such structures to have survived the passage of time.[5] The site, on top of a gentle hill, was deliberately selected by the anonymous architect to maximize both the cooling breezes and the fine views of the rolling valley. The design is simple but extremely refined. Although the perfect proportions of the façade have been spoiled somewhat by later additions, enough remains of the neoclassical detailing to suggest its former elegance.

4 Sugar was weighed in *arrobas*, a Spanish unit of measure equivalent to 25 Spanish pounds or eleven and a half kilograms.

5 Sugar plantations with their respective factories were known in Cuba as *ingenios* until the end of the Nineteenth Century. After the consolidation of many smaller plantations under a larger central administration, sugar factories became known as *centrales*.

The residence was flanked in the rear by twin pavilions that originally housed the kitchen and the household staff. Although no other buildings survive today, originally the plantation had many more. There were houses for the various administrators and supervisors, barracks for the slaves, warehouses and kitchens, all in addition to the different buildings where the separate steps of the manufacture were carried out. There was a mill for the extraction of the juice, boiler rooms for the production of molasses, and a separate building for the purification and molding of the final product. All these different structures were jointly known as the *batey*, a word that had been borrowed from the Indians.

Sugar was manufactured in the simple manner described above until the end of the Nineteenth Century. After 1868, various political and economic factors came together to bring about radical changes in the Cuban sugar industry. The independence movement had naturally disrupted life on the island and had affected all manner of trade. By the end of the century, many sugar factories were bankrupt, and American investors started buying the smaller enterprises. This development coincided with the introduction of new manufacturing methods to further purify and crystalize sugar into the white refined powder that is known today.

The new technology demanded an investment in machinery that was beyond the possibilities of most producers. The actual growing and harvesting of sugar cane became a separate enterprise in the hands of independent planters, whereas the manufacture of sugar became centralized in a reduced number of larger factories. This new system produced increased prosperity, due largely to an expansion into the North American market. Cuban sugar would eventually account for half of the world's production. The Spanish writer Vicente Blasco Ibáñez relates that, as a child, he imagined Cuba to be an enchanted place, "as in a fairy tale, where houses were made of caramel and candies could be picked from the ground."

Sugar came to dominate the Cuban economy almost totally.[6] At the time of the Cuban Revolution of 1959, ten percent of the population was directly employed in the industry. The secondary products of sugar manufacture were diverse. The fibrous pulp left behind after the extraction of the juice was processed into paper and livestock feed. Wine grapes could not be grown in

Right: the principal residence on the sugar plantation of Jesús Nazareno de Buena Vista near Trinidad is the only building to remain standing from the original complex.

Extreme right: this view of the entablature shows a section of the neo-classical detailing. The style remained popular in Cuba until the end of the colonial period.

Below: the sitting room of the Casa Cantero in Trinidad is an example of the taste of a rich Nineteenth-Century planter. Attracted by the prosperity of the sugar industry, many French and German immigrants settled in this area after 1840. The German name Kanter became Cantero in Trinidad.

6 In 1959, there were 161 factories producing sugar in Cuba. Of these, 117 were owned by Cubans, 40 by Americans and three by Spaniards. One was in French hands.

the Antillean climate, and all wine consumed in Cuba had to be imported. However, molasses could be fermented and distilled into rum, a liquor indigenous to the West Indies. Rum production is, in fact, one of the oldest of Cuban industries. Cuban rum formed an important part of the country's exports. Its excellence and unique character have been enjoyed around the globe.

The sugar industry suffered a serious setback at the time of the Cuban Revolution and the subsequent American embargo on all products manufactured on the island. Although neither the quantity nor the quality of Cuban production is at present what it once had been, sugar remains an important factor in the country's economy.

The impact of the sugar industry on Cuban life and culture has not been restricted to the economic sphere. The evolution of sugar plantations and their accessory complex of buildings was a uniquely Antillean achievement. Its success in integrating a wide range of residential and industrial structures within a defined and harmonious area would find an equivalent in the creation of industrial villages many years later. The design of sugar plantations in Cuba can be seen as one of the earliest examples of planned development in the New World.

Harvested sugar cane is brought to the mill in large containers.

CHAPTER SIX

The Sixteenth and Seventeenth Centuries
and the Threat of Piracy

By THE MIDDLE of the Sixteenth Century, just 50 years after the discovery of the New World, Spain had become unquestionably the greatest power in Europe. Charles V ruled over Spain, the Netherlands, Luxembourg, Sicily, Sardinia, Artois, and the Franche-Comté. He controlled all Habsburg possessions in Central Europe. Large parts of Italy were under his rule. The Philippine Islands, which had been named after his son and eventual successor, Philip II, were part of his territories. In addition, the Western Hemisphere, with the exception of Brazil, had become a Spanish domain. It was truly an empire on which the sun never set.

With the spread of Spanish possessions in the New World, the focus of activity gradually shifted away from the Antilles, which had been the first to be colonized. After 1518, Cuba became principally the base for further Spanish expansion in the Americas. The various expeditions that left from the island to attempt the colonization of Mexico have already been noted. The first fleet to explore the coast of Florida sailed from Havana in 1539 under the command of Hernando de Soto, who was Governor of Cuba. De Soto's wife, Isabel de Bobadilla, acted as his deputy during his absence. She was the first woman to hold such an important position in the New World.

Charles V was too busy in Europe to devote much time to the affairs of his colonies across the Atlantic, which he regarded primarily as a source of revenue. He had spent a great deal of money to secure his election as emperor, most of which had been borrowed from German bankers and had to be repaid. The ongoing struggle against Protestantism demanded the expenditure of large amounts of Spanish funds.[1] At the same time, Charles V was involved in a war with France which would prove extremely costly and would have im-

---

1 Martin Luther had started the Protestant Reformation in 1517, and Charles V became committed to halting the spread of what he considered Luther's heresy.

portant consequences for Cuba. Ever increasing supplies of gold and silver from the New World were required to pay for these various pursuits.

The conquest of the Aztecs in Mexico and of the Inca Empire in South America had made Spain the richest country the world had ever known. Fleets laden with wealth beyond measure crossed the Atlantic regularly to replenish Spanish coffers. Although Cuba's meagre supply of gold had been exhausted, the island nevertheless played an important role in this flow of treasure. Cuba is blessed with many spacious bays. The one at Havana is approached through a long and narrow entrance channel which makes it an outstanding natural harbor. Moreover, it is located literally at the threshold of the New World. Havana would be an obligatory port of call for Spanish ships and eventually would become the principal harbor of Spanish America.

The treasure flowing out of the New World soon attracted the attention of

60

La Punta is one of the two fortresses designed by Giovanni Battista Antonelli at the end of the Sixteenth Century to protect the entrance to the bay of Havana.

Spain's enemies. Maritime law had not yet been systematized in the Sixteenth Century, and it was considered perfectly permissible for the merchant ships of one nation to attack those of rival powers. Because of the ongoing hostilities between Charles V and the King of France, French ships in the New World had the approval of their monarch to capture and plunder any Spanish vessel. French corsairs became the bane of the treasure fleets.[2] As early as 1521, a ship sailing out of the Mexican port of Veracruz with part of Montezuma's riches was taken by Giovanni da Verrazano, a Florentine in the service of the French King.[3] Two years later, the Frenchman Jean Florin captured two ships transporting gold from Cortés to Charles V.

French corsairs attacked Cuba for the first time in 1537. Two Spanish ships loaded with Mexican treasure were pillaged while anchored in the bay of Havana. The French returned the following year to sack the city after having attempted to do the same in Santiago de Cuba. It is a curious fact that many of these corsairs were Huguenots. One of their leaders, Admiral Gaspard de Coligny, had suggested the foundation of French Protestant settlements in Brazil, where they could practice their religion without interference. Huguenots sailed regularly between France and the New World. Because Charles V had taken such an uncompromising stand against Protestantism, they derived special delight in attacking the ships that carried treasure to their nemesis, and did so with remarkable frequency and particular hostility.

A Huguenot commander named Jacques de Sores was to play an important role in the history of Cuba. In 1554, while returning from the fledging Huguenot colony in Rio de Janeiro, Sores occupied Santiago de Cuba and devastated the city. The following year he turned up in Havana, which still lacked adequate fortifications although it had become the capital and seat of the administration of the island. Sores appeared at the entrance of the harbor and took Havana by surprise. The head of the garrison, Juan de Lobera, retreated to the safety of the single fort in the city with some two dozen men. However, the governor, Gonzalo Pérez de Angulo, was barely able to round up half this number, and was forced to flee outside the city limits along with the rest of the population. Lobera was left unaided to fight French forces

---

2   A corsair or privateer was a private person undertaking maritime aggression under the authority of a monarch or government that would receive a share and occasionally all of the spoils. Corsairs attacked only ships flying certain flags. A pirate was someone who did basically the same, but for his own profit, and who indiscriminately attacked ships of all nationalities. Pirates were also called buccaneers.

3   Verrazano sailed into New York Bay in 1524, the first European ever to do so.

that numbered more than 200 men, and he surrendered the following morning.

Sores demanded a large ransom to withdraw from Havana, but Pérez de Angulo decided to attack the French by surprise while negotiations were still in progress. The governor's paltry forces consisted of some 40 Spaniards, 100 Africans and an equal number of Indians, none of them adequately armed. Although they managed to kill about 25 of the corsairs at the outset of the skirmish, their defeat was inevitable. In retaliation, Sores exacted an even more exorbitant ransom to spare the city. To drive his point home, he executed his prisoners in cold blood, including the women and children. Lobera was the only one left alive.

After holding Havana for almost a month, Sores realized that his demands would not be met. True to his word, he burned the city to the ground and destroyed all the surrounding plantations. The African slaves were taken away to be sold. Those who could not be contained on the ships were simply hanged, their corpses left to rot in the sun. The corsairs finally withdrew on the fourth of August 1555, leaving only ashes behind them.

The capture and destruction of Havana sent waves of consternation in all directions. Authorities on both sides of the ocean realized that a permanent occupation of the city by enemy forces would cause a serious disruption in the traffic between Spain and the New World. It was evident that Havana had been vulnerable to an alarming degree. The Council in Seville decided to reinforce the city's defenses, to station a permanent garrison and, in future, to appoint only military officers to the position of governor.[4]

Charles V died in 1558. Two years earlier, he had retired to a monastery after leaving the throne of Spain to his son, Philip II. Although the new monarch signed a peace treaty with France in 1559, Cuba continued to be attacked by pirates and privateers. In 1554, Philip II had married his cousin, Mary Tudor, Queen of England, where his inflexible Catholicism would make him an extremely unpopular figure. After Mary's death four years later, the Spanish monarch attempted to marry her successor, Queen Elizabeth I, but he was turned down.

Elizabeth's reign marked the emergence of England as a great naval power. Their rival commercial and religious interests resulted in a state of open hostility between Spain and England. The situation was complicated further

Philip II sent Antonelli to Cuba to improve the island's fortifications. The fortress of El Morro in Santiago de Cuba was part of his scheme to protect all the major cities and harbors.

4 All matters regarding Spanish America came under the jurisdiction of the *Consejo de Indias* in Seville.

in 1587 by the death of Mary, Queen of Scots, whose son James would be Elizabeth's successor. The Scottish Queen had disinherited her disloyal son and had named the King of Spain the rightful heir to the English throne.

Based on the edict that Pope Alexander VI had issued in 1493, Spain claimed exclusive rights to the New World. Starting with the Treaty of Cateau-Cambrésis, which was signed by Philip II and the King of France in 1559, Spain attempted to secure recognition of this position when negotiating peace treaties and agreements with other powers. However, Spain's rivals and adversaries in Europe saw matters in a different light, and the issue was never settled. The situation that developed was that within European waters and in the Atlantic Ocean up to the Azores, ships of different flags respected each other's rights to carry out trade. West of what came to be known as "the line of friendship," merchant vessels were free to attack Spanish fleets, and were most frequently encouraged to do so by their governments.

In 1567, an English privateer named John Hawkins appeared in the harbor of Veracruz with a shipment of African slaves and tried to sell them in open defiance of Spanish authority. Two of his ships were taken and sunk before Hawkins could escape on his third vessel, which was commanded by one of his subalterns, Francis Drake.[5] The capture and sinking of Hawkins' ships produced great indignation in England. Soon thereafter, the English adopted a policy of open reprisals against Spain.

Drake left England with a fleet of 25 ships and more than 2000 men in September 1585. He sailed to Hispaniola, where he took and pillaged Santo Domingo, and went on to do the same in Cartagena on the north coast of South America. The Spanish were certain that Havana would be the Englishman's next target and prepared for his attack. On his return to England, Drake sailed around Cuba and anchored his ships off the north coast of Pinar del Río, where he remained for a few days to take water and provisions.

In May 1586, the dreaded fleet finally appeared in view of Havana. However, 1000 Spanish soldiers were waiting in readiness, and Drake decided to keep going in the direction of Florida. His final foray against the Spanish, undertaken with the help of his former captain, John Hawkins, took place in 1595. It was a complete failure and would cost both men their lives. The English would have to wait more than 150 years before capturing Havana.

A bronze statue known as the Giraldilla surmounts the tower of the Castle of the Real Fuerza in Havana. It was cast in the Cuban capital in 1634 by Jerónimo Pinzón.

5 Francis Drake (1540–1596) was the first Englishman to circumnavigate the world. He plundered various Spanish settlements in South America before returning to London with spoils valued at more than two million pounds. He was knighted by the queen on board his flagship, the *Golden Hind*.

As a result of these attacks, Philip II initiated a plan to fortify the main Spanish ports in the New World. A new governor, Juan de Tejeda, arrived in Havana in 1589 accompanied by an Italian military engineer, Giovanni Battista Antonelli, who designed the massive fortress that still guards the approach to the bay of Santiago de Cuba. In Havana, Antonelli constructed the two forts that flank the narrow entrance to the harbor, *La Punta* and *El Morro*. By making it possible to protect Havana, Antonelli's work was of fundamental value in the future development of the city.

Cuba continued to be plagued by corsairs and pirates throughout the Seventeenth Century. Philip III had succeeded his father as King of Spain in 1598. Nine years later, in an attempt to improve the island's defenses, the king passed a decree dividing the government of Cuba into two sections, one administered from Santiago de Cuba and the other from Havana, which remained the capital. Approximately 20,000 people were living on the island at the beginning of the century, and half of them were concentrated in the area around Havana. Cuba's second city was Bayamo, situated safely away from the coast. Santiago de Cuba had one thousand inhabitants at that time.

Spain had continued her struggle against the Protestants with ever greater zeal and had attempted to suppress the spread of Calvinism in the Netherlands. The Dutch revolted against Spanish rule and declared their independence in 1581. Holland and Spain remained at war until 1648. During these years Spanish vessels were relentlessly pursued by the Dutch navy.[6] The Dutch West India Company had been started in 1621 to develop trade with the New World. That same year Philip IV assumed the throne of Spain.

The reign of Philip IV marks one of the most brilliant periods in the history of Spanish culture. Calderón de la Barca, Lope de Vega and Tirso de Molina, three of the greatest figures of Spanish literature, were all active during those years. The King was a great lover of the arts, and under his patronage Spanish painting attained its highest achievements. This was the time of Murillo and Velázquez, two of the finest painters in the history of Western art. Paradoxically, the reign of Philip IV also marks a period of political and economic decline in Spain.

The frequency of attacks on Spanish ships in the New World increased alarmingly during the decade ending in 1630, by which time Spanish naval power in the Caribbean had been reduced to almost nothing. The arrival of the

66

Right: this French bronze cannon remains in Santiago de Cuba as a reminder of the days when Cuban cities were attacked regularly by the enemies of Spain.

Far right: the bay of Matanzas, where the Dutch Admiral Piet Heyn captured a Spanish silver fleet in 1628. The spoils were worth twelve million florins, a great fortune at that time.

6 Hostilities between the two countries were halted for a period of twelve years starting in 1609.

Dutch after 1625 added to the ranks of French and English privateers active in the area. A squadron of Dutch ships dropped anchor directly in front of Havana in 1626, blocking all access to the port for one month and undertaking a careful study of the city's fortifications. The small fleet that had been organized to patrol the coast and protect Cuban settlements from attack was kept from leaving the harbor.

In 1628, two squadrons were sent to the Caribbean by the Dutch West India Company. The first squadron captured a Spanish fleet as it approached Havana and returned to Holland with their loot. The second anchored off the north coast of Pinar del Río to wait for the arrival of the treasure fleet from Veracruz. The Dutch were led by Admiral Piet Heyn, who had more than 3000 men on 31 ships under his command. In September of that year, the Spanish finally appeared within sight of Havana. With the Dutch blocking their passage, the commander had no choice but to continue in the direction of the bay of Matanzas, some 80 kilometers to the east, where Piet Heyn captured the entire fleet. The vessels had been carrying gold, sugar, indigo, and no less than 177,000 pounds of silver. The value of the spoils was a staggering twelve million florins. Although the Dutch sent a new squadron to Havana the following year, Piet Heyn's feat would not be repeated.

The activities of these privateers virtually crippled Spanish naval power and allowed the Caribbean to become the meeting place of buccaneers from every nation. Pirate attacks became the most serious problem facing Cuban cities. Santiago de Cuba was sacked in 1662 and Sancti Spíritus three years later. Pirates and privateers carried out more than 400 raids against Cuban targets in 1665 and 1666. Cities in the middle of the island were as much in danger of attack as coastal settlements. Puerto Príncipe was captured and sacked by the English buccaneer Henry Morgan in 1666 in spite of its location more than 50 kilometers from the coast.[7]

Cuba's resources were drained by these attacks. The export of tobacco and sugar had to be suspended, and the development of the island's economy came to an almost complete halt. Privateering was outlawed by the terms of the Treaty of Rijswijk in 1697. However, the activities of pirates and buccaneers, who did not acknowledge any law, proved almost impossible to control. Pirates would continue to plague the Caribbean throughout the Eighteenth Century and would be finally stopped only after 1825.

68

7   Puerto Príncipe is now called Camagüey.

This fortress was designed in 1738 by the Spanish engineer José Tontete to protect the entrance to the bay of Jagua, located on Cuba's south coast and valued by the colonists as the largest on the island. The city of Cienfuegos was founded here in the early Nineteenth Century by French immigrants from Louisiana.

CHAPTER SEVEN

The Eighteenth Century and the English Occupation

DESPITE THE DEVASTATION brought on by decades of continuous be-
leaguerment, the population of Cuba had grown to 50,000 by the beginning of the Eighteenth Century. The period immediately following the Treaty of Rijswijk was marked by an unprecedented surge in commercial activity. The cultivation of tobacco had increased, as had the production of sugar. However, this reprieve was not to last for long.

King Philip IV had died in 1665 and had been succeeded by his son, Charles II, who is known in Spanish history as Charles the Bewitched. The Habsburgs in Spain had been following a policy of consanguineous marriages to their Austrian cousins for several generations. Charles II suffered his entire life from a variety of congenital ailments that rendered him a weak and inefficient ruler. By the time of his second marriage in 1689, it had become evident that he would never be able to father an heir. Nonetheless, Spain remained a great power, and the matter of the Spanish succession became of vital importance to the whole of Europe.

On the basis of their descent from King Philip III of Spain, three different princes advanced claims to the Spanish throne. One of Philip III's two daughters had married Louis XIII of France and was the mother of Louis XIV. Her sister had married the Austrian Emperor and was the mother of Leopold I. A generation later, these two monarchs, Louis XIV and Leopold I, had married the two daughters of King Philip IV of Spain, who were sisters of Charles II.

In his will, Philip IV had named one of his daughters, the Infanta Margarita, who was the consort of Leopold I, as second in line of succession to the Spanish throne.[1] Her sister, the Queen of France, had been required to

---

1 Infante or Infanta is the title given to the sons or daughters of a Spanish monarch. The Infanta Margarita was painted by Velázquez several times. She is the central figure in his most famous canvas, *The Maids of Honor*, now in the Prado Museum in Madrid. Velázquez painted her portrait when she was two and again when she was eight. Both of these are in Vienna's Kunsthistorisches Museum.

renounce her rights of succession at the time of her marriage to Louis XIV.[2] The sole heiress of the Infanta Margarita and Leopold I had married the Elector of Bavaria and had given birth to a son, Joseph Ferdinand, in 1692. It was this little prince who had the most valid claim to succeed King Charles II of Spain.

Blood is not as powerful as politics when the fate of an empire is at stake. Despite the renunciation made by both his mother and his wife, Louis XIV claimed the throne of Spain for his grandson, the Duke of Anjou. The Emperor Leopold I did the same for one of his sons from his third marriage, the Archduke Charles, claiming that his daughter had bestowed her mother's dynastic rights on him. Although neither the Dutch nor the English could come forward with a candidate of their own, they observed the proceedings with keen interest. King William III of England, who had been born a Dutch prince, had regarded the French King with open hostility since Louis XIV's invasion of Holland in 1672, and was not inclined to accept the Bourbon claim.

However, neither William III nor Louis XIV wished to go to war over the issue of the Spanish succession, and they agreed to support Joseph Ferdinand. According to the terms of a treaty signed by England and France in October 1698, Spain and her overseas colonies would go to the Bavarian prince, whereas Spanish lands in Europe were to be divided between the Archduke Charles and the French Dauphin. The Spanish reacted with anger at the proposed dismemberment of their European possessions. King Charles II immediately made a will leaving his entire domains to Joseph Ferdinand. The death of the young prince in March 1699 was to render worthless both the Anglo-French treaty and the Spanish will.

The French and English knew that Charles II was dying and they wasted no time in signing a second treaty. According to the new terms, Archduke Charles was to get Spain, her overseas colonies, and the Southern Netherlands. The Dauphin would receive the remaining Spanish possessions in Europe. At the eleventh hour, the proponents of a Bourbon succession in Spain managed to convince Charles II to make another will. By the terms of this final document, Spain's undivided empire was left to the Duke of Anjou, who would become Philip V. One month later, in November 1700, Charles II was dead.

The first Cathedral on the island was constructed in Santiago de Cuba during the first half of the Sixteenth Century. The building was destroyed and rebuilt many times before being given its present appearance in 1922.

71

2　The consort of Louis XIV was the Infanta Maria Teresa. Her aunt and mother-in-law, the Infanta Ana, had also been required to renounce her rights to the throne of Spain when she married Louis XIII.

The Austrian Emperor, who had refused to endorse both Anglo-French treaties in the hope of gaining the entire inheritance for his son, was predictably indignant. Equally predictable was the decision of Louis XIV to break his treaty with England and endorse the accession of his grandson to the throne of Spain. From the beginning of his long reign, the French King's overriding ambition had been to establish France as the paramount power in Europe. With the help of many notable advisors and ministers, he had succeeded in increasing French authority and prestige to a remarkable degree. However, it was only after bringing Spain and her vast territories under the rule of a French prince that Louis XIV finally achieved his goal.

Dutch and English merchants had been engaged in many profitable enterprises in the New World. By going into partnership with Spanish associates, they had managed to circumvent the regulations that supposedly kept trade with Spanish colonies in Spanish hands. William III was eager to protect these Dutch and English mercantile interests. Colbert, the chief minister of Louis XIV, had started building shipyards with the idea of creating a large navy, which he considered an essential part of a French commercial empire.[3] It was certain that Philip V would favor the French.

French merchant ships started to call on Cuba from the very beginning of the new reign. A French naval squadron sent to protect the Spanish treasure fleet on its voyage across the ocean remained in Havana for five months in 1702. The presence of French troops had a brief but beneficial effect on the city's commercial and cultural life. Under their shadow, the pretense of the Spanish monopoly was temporarily abandoned. All manner of trade was allowed freely and openly for the first time, and business flourished. Up to that time, only Spanish sailors and officers had been permitted to mix with the population. These new visitors gave Cubans their first hint of the culture and sophistication that existed in France under Louis XIV.

The imbalance of power created in Europe by the accession of Philip V resulted in the the War of the Spanish Succession, which broke out in 1702 and would eventually involve every European power in a series of shifting alliances. The conflict was resolved in 1713 by the signing of the Peace of Utrecht, which

---

3   Jean Baptiste Colbert (1619–1683) was a French statesman who reformed French financial administration in the reign of Louis XIV. He encouraged the growth of industry and trade in an attempt to make France completely self-sufficient. Jean Orry, who was sent to Madrid by Louis XIV to restructure Spanish governmental administration, and who introduced the monopoly of tobacco in Cuba, was one of Colbert's disciples.

The Church of Santo Domingo in Guanabacoa was designed by Lorenzo Camacho and built between 1728 and 1748.

finally ended the monopoly long claimed by Spain in the New World. Among other important concessions, the English acquired exclusive rights to the slave trade with Spanish America.

Although the Peace of Utrecht would have disastrous results for Spain, the consequences for Cuba were mostly beneficial. The English had also gained the right to import 500 tons of merchandise yearly for sale in Spanish America. The ships that brought these wares were clandestinely restocked even as their cargo was being unloaded, with the result that uncontrolled quantities of goods were smuggled into Cuba.

After the Peace of Utrecht, Spanish policy was determined mainly by the need to maximize revenues from the New World. It was at this time that Philip V imposed the despised monopoly on tobacco. The Crown enacted numerous regulations to repress the traffic in smuggled merchandise. Despite all these efforts, smuggling continued to flourish on the island throughout the Eighteenth Century.

The commercial development of Cuba did not depend exclusively on illicit trade. Not only sugar and tobacco, but also great quantities of precious Cuban woods were exported to Europe. The shipyards that were started in Havana at this time gave further stimulus to the lumber industry and started an important internal transportation network. The development of the island was not limited to commercial pursuits. The University of Havana was established in 1728 and was followed by the foundation of the Royal Seminary of San Carlos y San Ambrosio in 1769. A public library was opened in 1793.[4]

A new governor, Juan Francisco de Güemes, had arrived in Havana in 1734. Within a year, he had organized a system of police detachments to impose his authority over the entire island and to safeguard public order. The governor was an ambitious and energetic man who immediately realized Cuba's potential. Five years after his arrival, Güemes formed a partnership to create the Royal Commercial Company of Havana. To secure royal favor, the king and queen were each presented with a share of five and a half percent in the new venture. The governor retained a controlling interest for himself.

Güemes' enterprise received the exclusive right to export all Cuban products, including tobacco. He was also allowed to import Spanish goods without paying duty. Among the conditions imposed on him was the obligation to keep a fleet of ten warships to combat smuggling. Profits were such that the

The University of Havana was founded in 1728. The buildings seen in this view date from the second quarter of the Twentieth Century.

4 This library, which still exists, was founded by the *Sociedad Económica de Amigos del País.*

value of shares had doubled by 1745. Stockholders were paid dividends of 31% after one particularly successful year.

After the death of Louis XIV in 1715, with the five-year-old Louis XV on the throne, French policy regarding England began to follow a more conciliatory line. However, the Spanish were still smarting from the humiliating terms of the Peace of Utrecht. Philip V's primary political objectives were the withdrawal of English slave merchants from Spanish America and the total eradication of the smuggling traffic they had created. To the indignation of the British, Spanish ships started to board English vessels suspected of carrying contraband. This policy would eventually cause a minor conflict between the two countries that is remembered by the humorous name of the War of Jenkins' Ear.

An English seaman called Robert Jenkins claimed that, in 1731, a Spanish captain had cut off one of his ears after boarding his ship. He appeared in the House of Commons in 1738 to tell his story, and brought his ear along. The sight of the mutilated organ caused such an uproar that the leading minister, Sir Robert Walpole, was forced to declare war on Spain. In 1740, an English force under Admiral Edward Vernon arrived in Havana and blocked the entrance to the harbor for two months. However, Güemes had taken precautions to defend the city, and Vernon withdrew.

Hostilities with England would come to an end after the death of Philip V in 1746. His son, Ferdinand VI, was a pacifist who followed a policy of complete neutrality. Smugglers from Jamaica and Haiti were allowed to operate in Cuban waters almost without restraint. An observer wrote in 1753 that there were warehouses in Havana for the storage of smuggled merchandise, and shops where it was openly sold. Contraband goods were offered in the streets even in public out of wheelbarrows. At the time of Ferdinand VI's death in 1759, approximately 60,000 people lived in Havana and its outlying area, more than in Boston, Philadelphia, or New York, which were then the three most populous cities in North America. The total population of Cuba at that time numbered 140,000.

Ferdinand VI was succeeded by his half-brother, Charles III. His reign would last three decades and would bring great prosperity to Cuba. Three years earlier, in 1756, a new war had started in Europe. The Austrian Empire had been invaded by the Prussian army under Frederick the Great. England had allied itself with Prussia against a league that included Austria, Sweden, Russia, Saxony, and France. Initially, Spain had remained neutral. However,

The city of Guanabacoa, located on the bay of Havana, was occupied by the English in 1762.
The Church of San Francisco adjoins a large monastery. Architectural elements are painted white to contrast with the yellow walls.

Charles III was ultimately persuaded to join the King of France in a Family Compact. In 1762, Spain was once again at war with England.[5]

The English had wanted to take Havana since the days of Sir Francis Drake. The new state of war gave them an excuse to try again. An English officer named Charles Knowles had visited Havana in 1756 and had made a detailed report of the city's fortifications. Based on this information, the English prepared their attack with great care. In March 1762, a fleet sailed for the West Indies under the joint command of Admiral Sir George Pocock and the Earl of Albemarle.[6] They were joined by additional English troops in the West Indies. Supplementary reinforcements had been promised from North America. When they had not arrived by the end of May, Pocock decided to proceed without them.

As it was, the fleet that attacked Havana was the largest military force ever to have been assembled in the New World up to that time. It consisted of more than 200 vessels and over 22,000 men. The normal route would have taken the English along the south coast of Cuba and around the Cabo de San Antonio. However, Pocock wanted to take Havana by surprise. The admiral brought his ships along the north coast of the island, a narrow and dangerous passage abounding with sand banks and other navigational hazards.

The armada arrived in front of Havana on the sixth of June. Due to the strength of the fortifications, Knowles had advised not to attempt a direct strike against the city. The English landed in the small cove at Cojímar, a few kilometers east of Havana, and proceeded west in the direction of the harbor. They took the village of Guanabacoa, which lies directly on the bay. From this position, facing the city, Albemarle mounted his attack on Havana's most important fortress, *El Morro.*

Fewer than 2000 professional soldiers were stationed in Havana at the time of the invasion. Five thousand members of the militia were added to this meagre number, plus 800 slaves who had agreed to fight after being promised their freedom. The grand total of Spanish forces consisted of fewer than 9000 men of diverse experience and dexterity. The English had more than twice this number of seasoned troops. Despite this disparity, the invaders encountered serious opposition. The siege of the city was to last two long months.

Captain Luis Vicente de Velasco was entrusted with the defense of *El*

---

5   This conflict is known as the Seven Years War.

6   Albemarle was a descendant of Arnold Joost van Keppel, a Dutch friend of King William III, who had ennobled him. Three Keppel brothers were part of the fleet that sailed from England in 1762.

Morro, which had been constructed by Antonelli more than 100 years earlier. Attempting to distract the attention of the Spanish, Albemarle ordered the bombardment of *El Morro* from the sea. However, Antonelli's retaining walls were too high for the ship's cannons to hit their target. The men under Velasco's command numbered no more than 400 but they resisted the unrelenting attack of the English for more than a month. Albemarle eventually dug a tunnel under the fortress and set off a large charge of explosives. Velasco was recovering from a wound when he heard the blast. Weak and delirious, the valiant commander left his bed to lead his troops, and was hit in the chest by an English bullet.

Albemarle's first concern after capturing *El Morro* was to save Velasco's life.. Escorted by an English officer, the Spanish captain was taken across the bay and handed over to the authorities in the city, where he died two days later. After his death, Velasco's extraordinary heroism and courage were widely recognized. His family received a title of nobility, and the king decreed that, in perpetuity, a vessel of the Spanish Navy would always be named in his honor.

Velasco was not the only hero to resist the advance of the English. One of the town councillors of Guanabacoa, José Antonio Gómez, played a leading role in organizing private resistance to the enemy. Groups of guerrillas under his command continuously engaged the English in debilitating skirmishes, which, indecisive as they were, nevertheless served the purpose of distracting their attention. More importantly, his exploits helped maintain the citizens' morale. Under his popular name, Pepe Antonio, he is remembered as a symbol of patriotic defiance.

Havana surrendered on the 12th of August 1762. The English took possession of the city the next day. The area under their control extended between Mariel, some forty kilometers west, and Matanzas, about twice this distance to the east. The value of the spoils taken is estimated at 650,000 Pounds Sterling. The Earl of Albemarle and Admiral Pocock each received 122,000 Pounds. In addition to this sum, Albemarle exacted large payments from the clergy in exchange for not plundering the churches.

The occupation of Cuba's largest and most important city seriously disrupted life on the island. The seat of government was transferred to Santiago de Cuba. All direct contacts between Spain and the former capital were discontinued. The English had appointed Albemarle's brother, Sir William Keppel, to the post of Governor of Havana. Keppel respected the authority of all municipal officers and did not oblige them to swear the customary oath of allegiance to the English King. A police force was organized to protect the population and control the mob of unruly sailors stationed in the city. Despite all of these efforts to gain the trust of the Spanish and Creoles, the English were never popular in Havana.

Commercial activity experienced a boom during the ten months of the English occupation. The harbor was declared open to all vessels from England and the English colonies in North America and the West Indies. Merchant ships loaded with all types of wares flocked to a port that had been closed to them for centuries. With the abolition of the trade monopoly of the Royal Commercial Company of Havana, Cuban merchants were able to sell their own products for higher prices than had been possible before. The trade in slaves also experienced a sharp increase. It is estimated that an average of 1000 Africans a month were brought to Havana during this period.

80

The Fuente de la India was part of a complex of public parks and wide promenades built just outside Havana's protective walls.

The war in Europe ended in February 1763. Under the terms of the Treaty of Paris, Spain ceded Florida to England in exchange for the return of Havana. A new governor was appointed by Charles III, Ambrosio Funes de Villalpando, Conde de Ricla. He arrived in July of that year to assume control. After the departure of the English forces, the city gradually returned to its former routine. However, the occupation had changed Havana in ways that would be as indelible as they were far-reaching in the future development of Cuba.

Just as the arrival of the French in 1702 had given Havana a taste of French culture, the presence of the English had introduced the city to a new mercantile philosophy. The traditional Spanish controls began to appear antiquated and exploitative. Cuban merchants, who had come in contact with the large and lucrative North American market, were no longer satisfied with the

Fragments like the one seen in this view are all that remain of the massive protective wall that once encircled the city of Havana.

restricted profits imposed on them by the official monopolies that had regulated all trade.

The defense of Havana had been conducted under the command of officers born in Spain. The Creoles, who made up the largest part of the population and had suffered the greatest losses, felt that they had been relegated to a secondary position and that their own efforts to save the city had been ignored. Pepe Antonio's death was imputed to the negligence of a Spanish officer. The fall of Havana was blamed on the ineptitude of the *peninsulares*, who certainly had made many serious mistakes. The Creoles felt that they deserved to have greater control over their own affairs.

Even before the English occupation, Spain had realized that changes in the administration of the island needed to be made. A new way of thinking known as the Enlightenment had developed during the Eighteenth Century. It discarded many of the traditions that had prevailed in Europe for generations and replaced them with a rational and scientific approach to all human endeavors. Enlightened thinkers advocated the expansion of industry and the establishment of free trade among nations, as well as the advance of education and the emancipation of the working classes.

No monarch deserves to be known as an enlightened ruler more than King Charles III of Spain. It was fortunate for Cuba that he occupied the throne precisely at a time when the island's population began to clamor for reform. The first governor appointed by him, Juan de Prado Portocarrero, had arrived in 1761 with orders to implement extensive changes in the administration. The English occupation intervened, and many historians have claimed that it actually accelerated these reforms. Be it as it may, Governor Ricla, who took over from the English in 1763, started a series of programs that eventually transformed the country.

Spain was naturally anxious to avoid a repetition of the English disaster, and 2000 soldiers arrived in Havana to reinforce the garrison. The reconstruction and enlargement of Havana's damaged fortifications was the first of Ricla's priorities. Three expert advisers arrived to help with the project. One was French, one German and the third Scottish. The fact that not one of them was a Spaniard is clear evidence of the King's more international outlook.[7]

Work on Havana's enlarged fortifications involved the efforts of over 4000

---

7 Ricla's advisers were Antoine Raffelin, whose task was to organize the cavalry, Augustin Kramer, who directed the construction of the new fortifications, and Alexander O'Reilly, who was put in charge of the armed forces.

The fortress of El Morro occupies the eastern side of the approach to the Bay of Havana. By 1766, the capital of Cuba was the most heavily fortified city in the Western World.

laborers for three years. In addition to the rebuilding of *La Punta* and *El Morro*, which had been seriously damaged, the project involved the construction of no less than five new fortresses. These included *La Cabaña*, which is located next to *El Morro* along the entrance to the harbor, as well as *El Príncipe*, a massive structure outside the city walls. By 1766, the capital of Cuba was the most heavily fortified city in the Western World.

This gigantic program was made possible by a ready supply of building material. The coastal area lying directly west of Havana is rich in deposits of a coralliferous stone that is excellent for construction work. Because of its high porosity, it acquires a patina which eventually gives it a look not unlike weathered travertine. Spanish builders used it extensively in the city. Most of the large religious, residential, and public structures in the old part of Havana were built with this local stone.

The funds to defray the considerable costs of the new fortifications were sent from Mexico, with the result that an extraordinary amount of wealth came into the city in a matter of a few years. Moreover, the thousands of workers and soldiers newly arrived in Havana all had to be clothed and fed. Ricla soon realized that it was impossible to supply the rapidly growing colony exclusively from Spain. He revoked the monopoly of the Royal Commercial Company of Havana, which ceased its operations forever. The harbor was declared open to ships of all nationalities. Within weeks, hundreds of vessels, many from North American ports, started to arrive in Havana. Foreign products, from American bricks to English cloth, regularly appeared in the city's shops. Commercial activity in Cuba during the first years of Ricla's administration actually surpassed the level it had attained under English rule.

The remaining years of the Eighteenth Century in Cuba were marked by a period of continuous growth. Louisiana had been ceded to Spain by France in 1763 and was governed from Havana. Traffic with Spain, which had been restricted to Seville and Cadiz since the early years of the colonial period, was extended to all other Spanish ports starting in 1764. The first Cuban newspaper, *La Gaceta*, started publication in the city that same year. It was soon to be followed by a second, *El Pensador*. A regular postal system was organized. Before long, it was expanded to include service to Spain. All letters from Central America and Santo Domingo were taken to Havana. Mail from the Philippines was carried across the Pacific Ocean to Mexico, and from there sent on to Cuba. Eventually, all communications between Spain and her colonies would be directed through Havana.

Cuba was blessed with a series of liberal governors who did a great deal to promote the welfare of the island. In 1766, Ricla was succeeded by Antonio María de Bucarely, under whose administration the work on Havana's fortifications was completed. After the introduction of apiculture in 1768, beeswax formed an important part of the island's exports. Coffee plantations were started around the same time. However, it was only after 1801, when many coffee planters left Haiti to settle in Cuba, that coffee would become an important part of the island's economic production.

Bucarely was followed by Felipe de Fondesviela, Marqués de la Torre. Under his rule, Havana acquired most of the monuments and public parks that still grace its historic center. Streets were paved and lighted. The *Plaza de Armas* was laid out. The elegant *Alameda de Paula* was built on the edge of the harbor as the earliest public promenade in the city. The new governor ordered the con-

The main entrance to the Royal Seminary of San Carlos y San Ambrosio, founded in Havana in 1769.

85

struction of the first public theatre. Within a few years, the citizens of Havana were enjoying regular seasons of theatrical performances and Italian opera. The *Teatro Tacón*, which was inaugurated in 1838, is the oldest theatre still in operation in the Western Hemisphere. The Havana Italian Opera Company traveled to New York as early as 1847. The great Italian tenor Enrico Caruso sang ten performances in Havana in 1920. He received an honorarium of $90,000, the highest fee that he was ever paid during his long career.

In 1774, when the first official census was conducted at the command of the Marqués de la Torre, 76,000 people lived in Havana. The entire country had a population of over 172,000 inhabitants. This number had grown to more than 272,000 by 1791, which represents an astonishing increase of 58% in just seventeen years. After the French took over Santo Domingo in 1795, thousands of Spanish settlers emigrated to Cuba.

This palace was built starting in 1766 on Havana's Plaza de Armas as the residence of the Capitanes Generales, governors of Cuba. It occupies the site of what had been the principal church of the city. The document that formally ended the Spanish occupation of Cuba was signed in this building in 1899. The inauguration of the first president of the Cuban Republic took place here in 1902. The palace served as the official presidential residence until 1920. It then became the seat of Havana's municipal government.

A postbox in the Plaza de la Catedral in Havana. The inscription reads 'internal and peninsular correspondence.' Most of the postal service between Spain and Spanish overseas possessions was channeled through Havana.

King Charles III had died in 1788. As a result of his enlightened outlook, Cuba enjoyed an unprecedented level of prosperity. After almost three centuries of Spanish domination, the island was beginning to develop a national identity of its own. The independence of the United States produced a marked expansion in trade between Cuba and the former English colonies in North America. These contacts were to lend momentum to the nascent liberation movement. Nonetheless, the long struggle for Cuban independence would continue until the end of the next century.

87

CHAPTER EIGHT

Architecture in Cuba

ALL WORKS OF ART inevitably reflect the physical surroundings of their creators, but architects are bound by the real world more than other artists. Climatic conditions dictate the number and dimension of windows. The location of a project restricts its size and form. Available materials largely determine the appearance of a building. Architecture is a product of the environment.

Spain encountered advanced civilizations in Central and South America. The Aztecs, the Mayas and the Incas were all great builders. A large number of their sophisticated constructions remains as evidence of their architectural and engineering skills. Spanish settlers in these areas incorporated a great deal of the native traditions in the design of their own buildings. The work of contemporary Mexican architects continues to reveal strong indigenous influences.

This was not the case in Cuba. The Tainos who were living on the island at the time of the colonization had attained only a primitive level of cultural development. Their rudimentary dwellings reflected their inability to work stone. Although not a single one of their structures has survived, the design of Cuban *bohíos* is based on earlier Taino prototypes. Their construction was extremely basic. The walls were held up by wooden supports driven into the ground. Canes were packed very tightly between these posts and held together with reeds. Palm leaves covered the roof. With a few variations, the *bohíos* still found in Cuba today conform to this simple design.

In the absence of an indigenous building tradition, Cuban builders had no choice but to draw on European sources for their inspiration. However, it would have been disastrous simply to replicate Spanish structures in a new setting. Buildings have to answer the needs of the people who occupy them. It was necessary to adapt European models to suit the physical conditions on the island. Cuban architects managed to do so with remarkable success. They

89

Trinidad was founded in 1514. The city has retained its colonial appearance to a remarkable degree. This view shows the Calle del Desengaño. The pink house with the long balcony is known as the Casa de Malibrán.

also contrived to use the restrictions imposed on them by the climate to create a new estheticism that is recognizably Cuban.

The methodical development of the earliest Cuban cities has been discussed briefly in an earlier chapter. The complexity and sophistication of colonial urban planning in Cuba can be fully appreciated in Trinidad, which was founded in 1514. Following Spanish tradition, houses were built around open central courtyards. Residential areas were similarly arranged around a series of squares. By subtly reflecting the plan of the houses, the urban layout harmoniously unifies communal and private areas of the city.

Public squares were planted with trees to provide shade. The sun shines with burning intensity in Cuba, and the need to control the light has always been a primary preoccupation of Cuban builders. Grills made of painted wood or wrought iron were fitted on the doors and large windows of all the houses. These grills filter the light while letting in the cooling breezes. They also supply an additional link between interior and exterior spaces. Their decorative designs enliven the plain surface of the whitewashed walls.

The churches in each residential area have belfries of unusual height. These towers served various purposes in addition to the obvious one of holding the bells that called the parishioners to worship. Their graceful outline added a pleasing elegance to the city. More important to the population was their value as landmarks. Neighborhoods were defined by their respective towers, which provided clearly visible orientational signs in an age when streets were not marked and the majority of the population could not read.

The architects who created Trinidad in the Sixteenth Century realized the need to divide cities into distinct sectors. Their prescient designs expressly provided the residents of each neighborhood with a sense of belonging to a local community and not to a large and shapeless urban mass. These same principles would continue to dominate city planning in the Twentieth Century.

Although Trinidad is unusual for its remarkable state of preservation, it is certainly not the only surviving example of colonial urban design in Cuba. The Spanish used the same formula in all parts of the island. Havana was first established on the south coast and was moved to its present location in 1519. According to tradition, the founders sought relief from the sun under a large ceiba.[1] They celebrated Mass and held a meeting of the city council. The spot is marked today by a small neoclassical temple known as the *Templete*.

---

1   The ceiba (Ceiba Pentranda) is a large tree indigenous to Cuba and the Antilles.

Many buildings in Havana were destroyed during the English occupation in the Eighteenth Century, but their reconstruction did not alter the original urban layout. The residential areas were built in a regular grid around a number of public squares. The *Templete* faces the Palace of the Governors across the *Plaza de Armas* in the heart of the oldest part of the city.

The squares of Havana were surrounded by wide colonnaded galleries. The design of these spacious loggias was based directly on models taken from Italian Renaissance books of architecture. However, their scale and form have been adjusted to suit the local environment. The climate in Cuba is both warmer and more humid than in any European country. Consequently, Cuban builders made these galleries taller and deeper than their European counterparts. The loggias of Havana offer cool protection from the sun and shelter from tropical rainstorms. Their shade provides an effective transition between exterior and interior spaces.

91

The Templete was erected in Havana in 1828 to mark the spot where the city was established in 1519.

Left: the bell tower of the Church of San Francisco is typical of Trinidad. Such towers served as landmarks in an age when there were no street signs and the majority of the population was unable to read.

Below: doors and windows are fitted with grills made of painted wood or wrought iron. The open passageways supply a visual link between indoor and outdoor areas.

Many of the buildings that face the public squares were designed around open courtyards enclosed by similar colonnaded galleries. The repetition of these forms in both communal and private areas creates a coherent and reassuring pattern throughout the city. Visual monotony is avoided by altering the scale to fit the setting. The result is an urban structure that is harmonious and unified.

The Sixteenth-Century houses that have survived in Cuba are modest utilitarian dwellings. Military buildings were much more important at that time, and a great deal more care was devoted to their design. The Castle of the *Real Fuerza* in Havana, which is the oldest in the city, is typical of early colonial military architecture. It was built over the ruins of a simpler fortress that had been razed by the French corsair Jacques de Sores in 1555.

The Castle of the *Real Fuerza* was erected between 1558 and 1577 by

Bartolomé Sánchez and Francisco Colona. The builders carefully selected an elevated site overlooking the entrance to the port, which the castle was meant to guard. The spacial mass is handled with great dexterity. Colossal walls made of the local collariferous stone rise out of a wide moat. The replacement of the original wooden drawbridge with a permanent approach has not diminished the impression of powerful inviolability. The castle was a comforting presence as well as a reminder of the power of the Spanish Crown.

The most interesting examples of domestic architecture in Cuba date from the Eighteenth Century. The *Casa de Calvo de la Puerta* on the Calle de Obrapía in Havana is a typical patrician residence of that period. It was built on the site of an earlier structure demolished at the time of the English occupation. The interior spaces were planned around two courtyards separated by a narrow passage and enclosed by wide covered galleries. All the main rooms open onto these patios. The dining room was placed in the passage between the two courtyards and opens onto both. This inspired feature keeps the room delightfully cool even in the hottest summer day. In creating a space that is perfectly adapted both to its setting and its function, the architect has fulfilled the fundamental purpose of his art.

The design of public buildings during the same period shows the influence of the baroque on Cuban architecture. The principles of the style had been formulated in Italy in the late Sixteenth Century and had been circulated throughout the world by the Jesuits, whose mother church in Rome, *Il Gesù*, had been the first baroque building. The richly undulating façade of the Cathedral in Havana was inspired by the Roman church of *San Carlo alle Quattro Fontane*, which is the work of the baroque architect Francesco Borromini.

Neoclassicism found great favor among Cuban builders. The introduction of the style on the island coincided with a period of great financial prosperity. Many ambitious neoclassical buildings were constructed in the course of the Nineteenth Century. The *Templete* in Havana has been mentioned. Most of the large suburban villas built around the city during this period were designed in the neoclassic style. The elegant main residence on the sugar plantation of *Jesús Nazareno de Buena Vista* near Trinidad was discussed in an earlier chapter. The *Teatro Sauto* in Matanzas, built in 1862, is one of the finest neoclassic structures in the country. The headquarters of the Matanzas fire brigade, erected in the purest neoclassic mode between 1897 and 1900, is evidence that the style remained popular with Cuban builders until the end of the colonial period.

95

Left: the Palacio Brunet in Trinidad. The tower of the Church of San Francisco can be seen in the background.

Page 96: the covered portico in front of the house of the Conde de Jaruco on the Plaza Vieja in Havana. Houses on the main squares were provided with sheltered galleries like this one to offer protection against the sun and the rain.

Page 97: the inner courtyard of the Palacio del Segundo Cabo on the Plaza de Armas in Havana. The colonnaded galleries reflect the design of the square outside. This repetition of forms provides a visual connection between interior and exterior spaces.

From the beginning of the Spanish presence on the island, Cuban buildings have reflected the influence of European architectural developments. Nevertheless, Cuban architecture is recognizably different from both its European models and its counterparts in Latin America. A distinct architectural look developed on the island as a result of the brightness of the Cuban light. Builders in many other parts of the world have had to deal with similar climatic conditions. Cuban architects, however, realized the ornamental potential of light. Through their creative handling of a simple problem, they created a unique architectural style.

Grills were used on windows to keep rooms dark. Their shadows created ornamental patterns on the outside walls. Cuban architects learned to control this effect by adjusting the grills' design and placement. The same principle was applied to other architectural elements. Cornices, architraves and volutes

Left: the Castle of the Real Fuerza in Havana was built between 1558 and 1577 on a raised site overlooking the entrance to the port. It is the earliest of the city's fortifications.

Below: the house of Calvo de la Puerta on the Calle Obrapía in Havana is designed around two inner courtyards surrounded by wide covered galleries.

were used to create strong shadows that animate both interior and exterior walls. By skillfully regulating their depth and projection, Cuban architects were able to integrate the effect of these elements in their total designs.

The principle was applied with great success in the design of the interior of the church of *San Francisco de Asís* in Havana, which dates from the Eighteenth Century. Massive pillars support a complex architrave that completely encircles the nave. Light enters through clerestory windows set above the architrave and creates a lively abstract pattern of zigzagging lines that enliven the otherwise stark space.

The manipulation of light and shadow became the foundation of a Cuban estheticism. The work of the modern Cuban artist Amelia Peláez reveals a similar preoccupation formulated in paint. Architecture continues to express it best.

Right: the Cathedral of Havana was built in the late Eighteenth Century. The design of the main façade was inspired by the work of the Roman architect Francesco Borromini.

Below: the dining room in the house of Calvo de la Puerta is open to both inner courtyards. The resulting space is perfectly adapted to both its setting and its function.

Left: the Teatro Sauto in Matanzas is one of the finest neoclassical buildings in Cuba.

Right: the Church of San Francisco de Asís in Havana is built near the port next to an open square.

Below: the strong Cuban light is used to create a decorative pattern of parallel lines which enlivens the interior of the church.

CHAPTER NINE

The Pursuit of Independence

THE GRADUAL DISINTEGRATION of the Spanish Empire in the New
World started with the loss of Santo Domingo in 1795 and ended with the
independence of Cuba more than a hundred years later. At the beginning of
the Nineteenth Century, the chaotic aftereffects of the French Revolution
were being felt throughout all of Europe. Spain was weak and badly governed.
The throne was occupied by Charles IV, a son of Charles III.[1] Totally unlike his
father in both temperament and intellect, Charles IV was feeble and indecisive. In 1793 he had been forced to declare war on the French Republicans by
the terms of the Bourbon Family Compact, which his father had signed 30
years earlier. Spain was invaded by the French and dragged into yet another
war with England. Meanwhile, the reins of government had been placed in the
hands of the Queen's lover, Manuel de Godoy.

The last of a series of able and efficient governors to be sent to Cuba, Luis
de Las Casas, had arrived in Havana in 1790. The years of his administration
marked the period of greatest prosperity that the island had ever known. After
the war with France started in 1793, direct contact between Spain and Cuba
practically ceased. Las Casas declared Cuban ports open to ships of all friendly
nations, and commerce flourished. The price of sugar attained levels never
before thought possible.

This period in the history of Cuba is almost totally dominated by the issue
of free trade. Spain reinstated commercial controls after the war with England
ended in 1795. The following year, Luis de las Casas was succeeded by the
Conde de Santa Clara. However, a new war with England had broken out. The
Spanish had no choice but to allow the resumption of free trade. Cuban merchants had been looking forward to another period of commercial growth, but

105

*The Parque Céspedes in Bayamo
is dedicated to the memory
of Carlos Manuel de Céspedes, leader
of the Ten Years War.*

---

1   The court painter of Charles IV was Francisco de Goya, one of the greatest of all Spanish artists. His
incisive portraits clearly show the weakness of the King's character.

the English imposed a naval blockade on Cuban ports. It became obvious that Spain's numerous wars would continue to disrupt progress on the island.

Santa Clara was followed by the Marqués de Someruelos, who arrived in Havana in 1799 with instructions to enforce the Spanish monopoly on trade with Cuba. The reaction among the Creoles was as negative as it was swift. Someruelos did not wish to start an insurrection and wisely decided to allow the continuation of free trade. He had been sent to Cuba primarily to defend the island against a possible attack from the United States. The Louisiana Territory, which was still governed at that time from Havana, adjoined the Mississippi River. The United States had been guaranteed unrestrained access to the river, but Spain had repealed this privilege in 1795.[2] It was essential to American mercantile interests to keep the Mississippi open to their ships. The Americans threatened war unless their rights were restored. However, Spain retroceded Louisiana to France in 1800. Three years later, the French sold the territory to the United States for the sum of 80 million French Francs.[3]

Although war with the United States had been averted, Someruelos knew that the cooperation of the Creoles would be of vital importance in the event of an invasion. Accordingly, his policies always followed a conciliatory line. After 1801, when the war with England was brought to an end, the Spanish again tried to reinstate their monopolies. Someruelos decided that, during his administration, these regulations would be enforced only if and when Spain became able to meet all of Cuba's needs.

A Venezuelan Lieutenant Colonel named Francisco de Miranda played a curious role in involving the United States in Cuban affairs. Miranda had come to Havana as an aide to the Governor. He was forced to flee to the United States after being accused of smuggling. Miranda devised a plan to secure the help of American and English forces to liberate not only Cuba, but all Spanish colonies on the mainland.

The spirit of expansionism was in the air in the United States. After securing Louisiana, the eyes of the American President, Thomas Jefferson, turned to the

2 The Louisiana Territory extended west from the Mississippi River. Spain also controlled the "two" Floridas. The present-day American State of Florida was known as "East Florida" in the Eighteenth Century. Although it had been ceded to England in exchange for Havana in 1763, it had reverted to Spain twenty years later. "West Florida" was the name given to the coastal area partly occupied today by the American states of Mississippi and Alabama. By commanding the mouth of the Mississippi, Spain effectively controlled traffic on the river.

3 Approximately fifteen million U.S. Dollars at that time.

The Church of San Salvador in Bayamo. The Bayamesa, national anthem of Cuba, was first sung here in 1868.

two Floridas and Cuba. Miranda was received in Washington by Jefferson and his Secretary of State, James Madison.[4] In 1809, an American envoy, James Wilkinson, arrived in Havana with a letter for Someruelos proposing a voluntary union between Cuba and the United States. Although Wilkinson was sent back with a negative reply, Jefferson remained confident that the island would one day willingly join its northern neighbor.

Colonial concerns were not among Spain's priorities during these turbulent years. In 1808, Charles IV had been forced to give up his throne in favor of his son, who became Ferdinand VII. Under the pretext of an interview, Napoleon lured father and son to Bayonne, very near the Spanish border, where he maneuvered to get an abdication from both monarchs. Ferdinand VII and his family were detained in France. Joseph Bonaparte, Napoleon's brother, was sent to Madrid to assume the throne. The Spanish had to start a war for their own independence.

The events in Spain caused a great commotion in Cuba. Someruelos decreed that the island was officially at war with France. However, after the initial shock had died down, Cubans realized that, for the first time, they were able to manage their own affairs with little interference from Spain. This short period of relative autonomy made most Creoles finally aware of the fundamental failings of their relationship with Spain. The country's welfare and prosperity were being affected by conflicts that had no direct significance for Cuba and over which the island had no control. Nationalist sentiments were beginning to spread throughout other Spanish colonies and these were equally vigorous in Cuba. Even during the prosperous last years of the Eighteenth Century, many people had grown dissatisfied with Spanish rule.

Francisco de Arango y Parreño was a Cuban planter and economist whose efforts to secure the free importation of slaves have already been mentioned. It was Arango's belief that Cuba was not a colony, but a province of the monarchy, and that, as such, it deserved the right to control its destiny. At the time of Joseph Bonaparte's assumption of the Spanish Throne, legislative assemblies had been formed in the various provinces of Spain. In 1808, under Arango's influence, Someruelos proposed the formation of a similar assembly in Havana. Opposition to the plan came from the three autonomous agencies that existed in Havana to control the Treasury, the Navy, and the tobacco monopoly. These three offices were answerable directly to the Crown. The men who

Santiago de Cuba was the site of an important battle between Spanish and American forces in 1898. The city is built on a series of hills that surround the bay. This view shows the Calle Padre Pico.

4 In 1809, Madison succeeded Jefferson as fourth President of the United States.

ran them had surrounded themselves with privileges and powers that they were jealous to guard. After conducting a defamatory campaign against Arango, the *peninsulares* rejected the proposed assembly.

Cuba was granted the right to be represented in the Spanish Parliament by a Royal Decree of 1810. In spite of this development, the antagonism between the Creoles and Spain continued to grow. Because the colonies had the right to be represented by just one delegate each, it was clear that Spanish provinces would be guaranteed a majority of votes. It seemed unlikely that the colonists would receive any of the concessions they had been seeking. To the surprise of everyone in Cuba, free and direct trade was authorized between Spanish America and all European countries and their colonies under the terms of a later decree. This decision, which might have retarded the Creoles' pressing demands for independence, was immediately rescinded.

During the years of his exile in France, Ferdinand VII had become the rallying cry of nationalist feelings. In 1812, a liberal constitution was proclaimed in the name of the absent King. Two years later, as soon as he had been reinstated to his throne, Ferdinand revoked the constitution in an attempt to establish absolute rule. The rest of his reign was marked by continuous uprisings. In his dealings with Cuba, however, Ferdinand VII showed remarkable political astuteness.

Although most of Spanish America was in a state of open revolt by 1814, Cuba had remained loyal to Spain. Shipments of both funds and troops had been sent to Ferdinand VII from the island. The King was anxious to secure Florida and to recapture at least a part of his lost empire. He decided to turn Cuba into the base for these military operations, and realized that he could do so only if had the good will and cooperation of the Cuban population. In 1816, a new governor, José Cienfuegos Jovellanos, arrived in Havana laden with honors to distribute among the population. Land grants, titles of nobility, medals and decorations were given out in great profusion. Arango was appointed to the post of Permanent Advisor to the Council of the Indies. The controversial tobacco monopoly was abolished in 1817. Free commerce with all nations was legalized the following year.

It was fortunate for Ferdinand VII that his reign coincided with a period of world economic growth. The price of sugar jumped to three times the level it had been in 1807, and coffee sold for five times the amount it had brought six years earlier. In spite of the general prosperity that ensued, the sharp distinctions between Creoles and *peninsulares* continued to cause discontent.

The Americans destroyed the Spanish fleet as it was trying to escape from the large Bay of Santiago de Cuba.

The census conducted in 1817 revealed that the population of the island had risen to more than 630,000 inhabitants, a growth of 132% in 26 years. Nevertheless, the Crown wanted to encourage even greater numbers of Spaniards and other Europeans to settle in Cuba. Each prospective immigrant was offered free passage, a grant of arable land, tax exemptions, and various other financial incentives. In 1819, the city of Cienfuegos was founded by French colonists from Louisiana. By 1827, the population had increased to over 700,000.

The fact that the independence movement took such a long time to reach its culmination in Cuba can be explained partly by the arrival of these new immigrants. Spain's other possessions in the Americas had large indigenous populations and could count on thousands of dissatisfied Indians to combat the Spanish. However, most of Cuba's native Tainos had been killed during the first years of the colonization. With the exception of the Africans, who were held in bondage, the majority of the Cuban population was made up of either Spaniards or their descendants. The feeling of loyalty to Spain among both groups remained very strong.

Three distinct political factions existed on the island. The most conservative were the reformists, who did not wish a break with Spain but only certain reforms in the system. A second group consisted of annexionists who sought to unite Cuba to the United States. The most radical were the separatists, who wanted nothing short of complete independence for the island.

The political situation in Spain continued to deteriorate. The liberals staged an unsuccessful revolution in 1820 which was followed by greater repression. The King's death in 1833 resulted in more disturbances. Ferdinand VII had discarded Salic Law to make it possible for his only daughter to succeed him.[5] The conservatives believed that the rightful heir was Ferdinand's brother, the Infante Don Carlos. When Isabella II ascended to the throne with the support of the liberals, civil war broke out in Spain.[6]

By the time that Miguel de Tacón assumed the governorship of Cuba in 1834, the independence of the former Spanish colonies in the New World was an established fact. Florida had been sold to the United States in 1819.[7] Four years later, the American President, James Monroe, had declared that Euro-

112

---

5 Salic Law excluded women from the succession to the throne. It was followed by the Bourbons in France and had been introduced in Spain only at the time of the accession of Philip V in 1700.

6 This conflict, which intermittently went on for years, is known as the Carlist Wars.

7 "West Florida" had been in American hands since 1810.

The Basílica
de Nuestra Señora del Cobre
near Santiago.

pean powers would no longer be permitted to interfere with political developments in the Americas.[8] There were to be no more schemes to recapture the lost Spanish Empire, and therefore there was no need to conciliate the Creoles. Spain was eager to retain Cuba, and willing to use any means to do so.

The years of Tacón's rule were characterized by increased political repression. In 1837, Cuba was denied the right to be represented in the Spanish Parliament. Spain decided that the government of the island would be carried out by special laws. Since such laws were never formulated, this decree granted the governor arbitrary control over Cuba's affairs.

Tacón was a rigid and inflexible man who not did not hide his disdain for the Creoles, regardless of class or social position. Cubans universally despised him in return. The discontent that had been simmering on the island for decades became focused on the figure of the governor, who was seen as the embodiment of everything that was wrong with Spanish rule. It could be claimed that Tacón unwittingly aided the cause of independence by uniting public opinion against him.

American political events also had an effect on the situation in Cuba. A strong anti-slavery movement had developed in the North of the United States, whereas the South remained firmly in favor of slave labor. This conflict would eventually result in the American Civil War. Southern states viewed the acquisition of Cuba as a way to expand slave territory and thereby offset the anti-slavery faction in Congress. Unsuccessful attempts to purchase Cuba from Spain were made during the administrations of Presidents Franklin Pierce and James Buchanan.

Many influential Cubans were in favor of a union with the United States. The noted Cuban novelist Cirilo Villaverde was among them.[9] Perhaps the most active of the annexionists was an army General called Narciso López, who had left his native Venezuela for Cuba in 1823, had distinguished himself in the Carlist Wars, and had served as Governor of Trinidad until 1843. His plan was to evict the Spanish from Cuba and then to seek admission to the American Union. He had to flee to the United States in 1848. That same year, with aid from the Americans, López organized the first of three filibustering

This monument in Havana is dedicated to Máximo Gómez, who was one of the two principal military commanders during the Cuban War of Independence. The Presidential Palace can be seen in the background.

8 This proclamation, which is known as the Monroe Doctrine, has remained a fundamental part of American foreign policy.

9 Cirilo Villaverde (1812–1894) was the author of *Cecilia Valdés*, which was published in 1839 and is considered the first Romantic novel written in the New World. His other works include *Dos Amores* and *El Penitente*.

expeditions to Cuba, all of which were to be unsuccessful.[10] He was captured by the Spanish and executed in 1851. In spite of his ultimate defeat, Narciso López left an indelible mark on Cuban history. The standard that he designed and flew during his campaigns was adopted in 1901 as the national flag of Cuba.

Although the United States and Spain were not officially at war, the situation between the two countries was very tense. In 1854, an American merchant ship called the *Black Warrior* was seized and held by Spanish authorities in Havana on the excuse that the captain had violated customs regulations. The capture of the *Black Warrior* created a furor in the United States. Southern legislators proposed an immediate declaration of war on Spain and an annexation of Cuba. The crisis was eventually resolved in a peaceful manner after the ship was allowed to sail from Havana.

A few months later, in October 1854, three of the leading American diplomats serving in Europe held a meeting in the Belgian city of Ostend to discuss the situation in Cuba. They included Pierre Soulé, who, as American envoy in Madrid, had been asked to investigate the possibility of buying Cuba from Spain. The other two were John Mason and James Buchanan.[11] The three diplomats, who were all pro-slavery Democrats, issued what has come to be known as the Ostend Manifesto. This document, which was addressed to the American Secretary of State, described the potential value of Cuba to the United States and strongly recommended its acquisition by any means. In the event that Spain should be unwilling to sell the island, the manifesto went on to say that Americans were justified "by every law, human and divine," in forcing it out of Spanish hands. Although the Ostend Manifesto was rejected at once by the government in Washington, its aggressive expansionist language caused considerable concern in Europe. It remains a useful reminder of how important the Cuban question had become for the United States.

Spain was aware of the seriousness of the situation in Cuba, and mindful of how precarious Spanish domination of the island had become. However, nothing was done to bring about the necessary changes. The public debt had

10 The term filibuster is derived from the Spanish *filibustero*, which is itself a corruption of a Dutch word, *vrijbuiter*, meaning freebooter. In the Seventeenth Century, filibustering was applied to the activities of pirates. In the Nineteenth Century, the expression was used pejoratively to describe an independent military campaign organized and led by private individuals against territories that were officially not at war with their own countries, such as the many American expeditions against Texas.

11 Mason was the American envoy in Paris, and Buchanan, who would become President of the United States three years later, held the same position in London.

The tomb of José Martí in Santiago de Cuba.

risen alarmingly, and taxes were increased as a result. Far more grievous to the Creoles was the fact that Cuba remained unrepresented in the Spanish Parliament. At the end of 1865, the Spanish Government decided to form an informatory assembly to compile a list of recommended reforms. Beginning in October 1866, the sixteen Cuban members of the informatory assembly met with government representatives in Madrid. They returned to Havana seven months later, having obtained no concessions.

The separatists were more convinced than ever that an armed uprising was the only means to gain independence from Spain. The area around Bayamo in the province of Oriente, which was populated mostly by separatist Creole planters, was a hotbed of revolutionary activity. One of their leaders was a wealthy planter named Francisco Vicente Aguilera. Many secret meetings were held during 1867 and 1868 to discuss the best way to proceed. Aguilera was fully in favor of starting a revolution, but believed that it needed to be planned very carefully. A planter from Yara, located some 50 kilometers to the west of Bayamo, was of a different mind. He felt that the moment was right for action. His name was Carlos Manuel de Céspedes.

By August 1868, the Spanish authorities were beginning to suspect that an insurrection was planned. Céspedes was a lawyer as well as a planter, a learned and cultivated man who wrote poetry and loved music. He was also a gifted orator who was able to convince many of his fellow conspirators that immediate action was required. They selected the 14th of October as the date to start their uprising. However, the governor in Havana had learned of their plan, and sent a telegram to his deputy in Bayamo ordering the immediate arrest of Aguilera, Céspedes, and all the other leaders of the insurrection. Fortunately, the local telegram operator leaked the message to Céspedes.

The news of their impending arrest spread quickly among the revolutionaries, and many of them found their way to *La Demajagua*, the Céspedes estate near Yara. Shortly after dawn on the tenth of October 1868, Céspedes proclaimed the independence of Cuba and declared war on Spain. Immediately thereafter, he called his slaves together and granted them their freedom. The proclamation made by Céspedes that morning, which is remembered as the *Grito de Yara*, launched the Ten Years War. It was to be one of the longestt and bloodiest conflicts ever fought in the New World.

Initially, the insurgents were few and badly armed. A week later, the rebel army numbered more than 1500 men. The capture of Bayamo on the 20th of October gave an extraordinary boost to the revolutionaries' morale. Céspedes

Right: the Church of the Holy Trinity in Trinidad was built in the Nineteenth Century.

Page 120: the tricolor standard designed by Narciso López and flown by his men during their filibustering expeditions was adopted in 1901 as the Cuban national flag. This view shows the flag being flown from the balcony of the Palacio del Segundo Cabo in Havana.

Page 121: the Capitol in Havana.

118

was given a hero's welcome by the delirious population. A patriotic song, *La Bayamesa*, was composed by a local poet named Perucho Figueredo. This rousing hymn was sung by the troops as they went into battle. After independence, *La Bayamesa* was adopted as the Cuban national anthem.

The revolt spread very quickly through the eastern part of the island. General Máximo Gómez joined forces with Céspedes. He was an experienced soldier who had served with the Spanish Army both in his native Santo Domingo and in Cuba. Large areas of the province of Oriente were soon under his control. Although Aguilera remained weary of Céspedes' leadership, he also joined the revolutionaries. Calixto García, Antonio Maceo and Tomás Estrada Palma also played important roles during the war.

Just weeks before Céspedes had declared the independence of Cuba, Isabella II had been deposed in Madrid. The Spanish Parliament established a constitutional monarchy and would later offer the throne to an Italian prince.[12] In spite of the uncertainty of the political situation in Spain, the Governor of Cuba, General Francisco Lersundi, was determined to crush the revolution with uncompromising harshness. Great numbers of Spanish soldiers were dispatched to the eastern part of the island, where rebel activity was concentrated.

In April 1869, the leaders of the rebellion convened a constituent assembly in Guáimaro in the Province of Camagüey. They drew up and approved the first Cuban constitution and elected Céspedes president of the new republic. The advance against the Spanish, which had been so swift in the early months of the campaign, slowed down during the following two years. Dissent among the revolutionaries resulted in increased opposition to Céspedes, and he was deposed in 1873. The great patriot, who had sacrificed everything for the cause of independence, was killed by Spanish soldiers a few months later. His son and namesake would become president of an independent Cuba in 1933.

After six years of exile, Alfonso XII was proclaimed King of Spain in 1874. One of the men who had engineered the monarch's return to Madrid was a powerful army general named Arsenio Martínez Campos. He had been in Cuba between 1869 and 1872 to lead the offensive against Céspedes. In 1876, he was again sent to Havana, this time for the express purpose of putting an end to the insurrection. Martínez Campos assumed command of the Spanish armed forces in Cuba, which numbered 250,000 soldiers.

123

Left: the Malecón follows the coast west of the bay of Havana and is one of the city's main boulevards. These buildings date from the first years of the Twentieth Century.

Below: the history of the Palace of the Governors on Havana's Plaza de Armas is outlined on this plaque.

12 This was Amadeus, Duke of Aosta, who reigned between 1870 and 1873.

Surprisingly, the General's policy was decidedly pacifist. The continuation of the war had produced a certain weariness among the population of the island. Martínez Campos found the political climate propitious to a peace settlement. In February 1878, due largely to his efforts, Spain and Cuba signed the Pact of El Zanjón, which officially ended hostilities between the two nations. However, some of the rebel leaders in Oriente, notably General Antonio Maceo, were unwilling to stop fighting until independence had been won. It was only after Maceo had gone into exile at the end of May of that year that his troops laid down their arms. The Ten Years War was finally over.

The cost in human life had been enormous. It is estimated that over 200,000 people had been killed. Spanish troops had committed appalling atrocities against the civilian population, even in areas where there had been no revolutionary activity. Property damage throughout the island simply could not be measured.

Although the Ten Years War did not result in independence, the mere factt that Spain had signed a peace treaty with Cuba was an acknowledgement of national autonomy. Under the terms of the Pact of El Zanjón, Cuba was promised sweeping political reforms. The island was granted direct representation in the Spanish Parliament, an end to the incarceration of political prisoners, and recogniniton of the freedom of those slaves who had fought with the rebels. The promised political reforms were never implemented.

Cuba entered a period of relative peace which was to last seventeen years, but the spirit of the revolution had not been laid to rest. The Cuban writer and patriot José Martí referred to this phase in the pursuit of independence as the time of "turbulent repose." Martí was a remarkable figure by any standards. He was born in Havana in 1853. One year after the outbreak of the Ten Years War,, when he was a young man of sixteen, Martí published his first patriotic newspaper, *La Patria Libre,* which led to his arrest and imprisonment for revolutionary activities. He served six months of hard labor, and was exiled to Spain in 1871. He was eighteen years old at the time.

He studied law at the University of Saragossa and received his degree in 1874. The following year he left Spain for France, then moved initially to Mexico and subsequently to Guatemala. He returned to Cuba in 1878, only to be exiled again one year later. He eventually settled in New York, where there was a sizable Cuban colony, and where he devoted the rest of his life to the cause of Cuban independence.

Martí was a prolific essayist whose work regularly appeared in the New York

The Paseo del Prado.

*This monument in Havana
commemmorates the destruction of
the American battleship Maine
in 1898. The American eagle which
originally crowned it
was toppled after the Revolution
of 1959.*

Sun as well as in newspapers in South America. Through his frequent contributions to *La Nación* of Buenos Aires, his name became known throughout the whole of the Spanish-speaking world. In addition to his essays, he wrote poetry, novels and short stories. Martí's innovative literary style has earned him a place in Spanish letters as one of the precursors of the modernist movement.

There were large numbers of Cuban exiles living in New York, Tampa and Key West. Martí kept in touch with all of them. By his writings as well as through his oratory, he was the force that bound these groups together and that would eventually galvanize them into action against Spain. Martí was the leader of the group that founded the *Partido Revolucionario Cubano* in 1892. The main objective of the party was to plan the invasion of Cuba.

All the major leaders of the Ten Years War would take part in the projected campaign. At the end of January 1895, Martí left New York for Santo Domingo. It had been decided to start military action on the 24th of February. On the appointed date, fighting broke out simultaneously in various places on the island. The Cuban War of Independence had begun.

On the eleventh of April, in the company of Máximo Gómez, Martí arrived in Cuba. Antonio Maceo, who had refused to accept the Pact of El Zanjón, had arrived the same day. On the fifth of May, at a sugar plantation called *La Mejorana,* Maceo met with Martí and Gómez to plan their strategy. On the 19th of May, Martí and Gómez encountered Spanish troops on an open plain near the spot where the river Contramaestre flows into the Cauto. The area is known as *Dos Ríos.* Martí was not a military man and had no experience in combat. Nevertheless, he insisted in joining the battle. He was the first casualty of the day.

As had been the case in 1868, the war had started in Oriente. The southeastern area of the province, which included Santiago de Cuba, was controlled by Major General Guillermo Moncada, who was a descendant of African slaves, as was Maceo. The insurgents started their march to the west in October 1895. In spite of heavy opposition from the Spanish, the liberating army moved inexorably across Cuba under the command of Gómez and Maceo. The invasion reached the westernmost province, Pinar del Río, by January 1896. The entire island was in rebel hands. Martínez Campos, who had returned to Spain in 1879, had been recalled to Cuba in 1895. This time, however, his lenient policies could not contain the insurrection.

In 1896, one year into the war, Martínez Campos was replaced by a new governor, Valeriano Weyler, who had been charged with the eradication of

the rebellion at any cost. Weyler devised a cruel and inhumane plan to cut off supplies to the rebels. This event is known in Cuban history as the *Reconcentración*. The governor ordered the forced removal of the entire rural population from their lands and homes. Thousands of defenseless peasants were herded into the fortified cities. Without adequate food or shelter, hundreds of people died. The news of the sufferings caused by Weyler's brutality brought condemnation from the United States. In 1897, Weyler was relieved of his duties and called back to Spain.

Weyler's replacement, General Ramón Blanco, arrived in Cuba with an offer of autonomy from the Spanish government. Five prominent Cubans were selected to form an independent Council of Ministers. They assumed their duties at the beginning of January 1898. However, the moment for these measures had passed. Cuba had been fighting a war against Spain for almost 30 years. The insurgents knew that the struggle was almost won. Nothing short of complete independence would satisfy them now.

The United States had wanted to annex Cuba since the days of Thomas Jefferson. The fruit was finally ripe and ready for picking. On the pretext of safeguarding American nationals on the island, the United States battleship *Maine* arrived in Havana at the end of January 1898. It dropped anchor off the coast directly to the west of the entrance to the harbor. It remained there, in full view of the city, for almost three weeks. On the evening of the 15th of February, the *Maine* was sunk by a mysterious explosion. Two hundred sixty-six Americans died.

The cause of the blast was never determined. Spanish authorities claimed that it had been the result of an accidental explosion in the ship's ammunition storeroom. The Americans blamed it on a submarine mine. Regardless of the reason, the sinking of the *Maine* caused an uproar in the United States. Certain that the disaster had been the work of Spain, Americans adopted "Remember the Maine" as a patriotic slogan during the Spanish-American War.

The Spanish were eager to avoid a conflict with the United States. However, American public opinion demanded a war. Although Spain had ordered a suspension of all hostilities against the rebels on the tenth of April, the next day President William McKinley requested authority to intervene in Cuba. The Congress passed a resolution demanding the withdrawal of Spanish forces from the island. The enlistment of American troops was ordered on the 22nd of April. Two days later, Spain declared war on the United States.

The Centro Asturiano in Havana was one of the social organizations that served the large number of Spaniards who chose to remain in Cuba after independence.

The American navy moved quickly. A blockade of the harbor of Santiago de Cuba was in place by the 28th of May. Five weeks later, the Spanish fleet, which had been docked there, was destroyed while attempting to escape. American forces landed near Santiago and attacked the city. Theodore Roosevelt, who would become President of the United States in 1901, led the charge on San Juan Hill.

The outcome of the war had never been in question. The surrender of Santiago de Cuba on the 16th of July made it obvious to the Spanish that it was pointless to continue the fight. An armistice was signed on the 12th of August. The final peace was formalized in Paris on the 12th of December 1898. Four hundred years of Spanish domination in Cuba had come to an end.

CHAPTER TEN

The American Intervention and the Start of the Republic

THE TREATY OF PARIS ended the Spanish-American War. Spain was made to withdraw from Cuba and renounce all further claims to sovereignty over the island. In spite of these terms, the independence of Cuba was not assured. The treaty also provided for the establishment of an American military government in Havana.[1] The United States would occupy Cuba with the intention of protecting the lives and property of the population and completing the pacification of the country. Cuba had not been consulted about the treaty.

On the first of January 1899, General John R. Brooke officially took possession of the island. It was understood that the American presence was to be temporary. However, the intentions of the United States regarding Cuba had never been clear, and many Cubans were concerned. As it was, the American military occupation would last for a period of 41 months and would result in great improvements to the country. It would also have a bitter aftermath.

In December of that year, it was announced that Brook would be replaced by Captain Leonard Wood. The news was greeted with widespread approval. Wood had contacts with many high-ranking Cubans, both civilian and military. He had received a degree in medicine from Harvard University in 1884 and had come to Cuba with Theodore Roosevelt in 1898. After taking part in the attack and capture of Santiago de Cuba, Wood had remained in the city as its military commander. He was both respected and liked.[2]

Wood remained in office from December 1899 until the end of the American military occupation in 1902. During these years, most government posi-

---

1   The United States obtained substantial gains as a result of the Spanish-American War, which had lasted only four months. Puerto Rico and Guam became American possessions. The Philippine Islands were surrendered by Spain against a payment of twenty million U.S. Dollars.

2   Wood was later promoted to Major General. In 1920, he tried to get the Republican nomination for President but was unsuccessful. He ended his career as Governor General of the Philippines.

tions were filled by native Cubans. Sanitary conditions in the country had sunk to a deplorable level in the period directly following the war. As a doctor, Wood considered the improvement of sanitation one of his first priorities. A council was organized to supervise all matters regarding public health. The ultimate eradication of yellow fever on the island was perhaps the most significant achievement of Wood's administration.

Yellow fever is an infectious disease that causes high fever and jaundice, and in most cases leads to death. It used to be endemic to tropical areas from the South of the United States to Mexico, Central America, and the Caribbean Islands. Epidemics of yellow fever caused thousands of casualties every year. There was no known treatment for the disease.

In 1881, a Cuban doctor named Carlos J. Finlay had discovered that yellow fever was carried by a mosquito.[3] However, the Spanish authorities had done nothing about his findings. Wood immediately organized a committee to study the problem. In 1900, a team of experts led by an American doctor, Walter Reed, arrived in Havana. After confirming Finlay's theory, they proposed a campaign to exterminate the mosquito. Wood immediately put it into action throughout the country.

Wood was an efficient and dynamic administrator. He reformed the judicial system and created the Cuban Supreme Court. Government operations were centralized. A comprehensive reorganization of both the postal service and the customs department was undertaken. Public education was vastly improved. One thousand three hundred elementary school teachers were sent to Harvard University for training. During Wood's administration, almost 2000 public schools were in operation in every area of the island.

An eminent Cuban professor, Enrique José Varona, was named to the office of Secretary of Public Instruction. Under his guidance, the system of higher education was completely revised. The curriculum of secondary schools was expanded. Important new faculties were started at the University of Havana, including Architecture and Electrical Engineering. The School of Medicine was enlarged.

Wood went to Washington in 1900 to meet with President McKinley and his Secretary of War, Elihu Root. On his return to Cuba in July of that year,

133

Window on the Church of San Francisco in Santiago de Cuba.

3   Carlos J. Finlay (1833–1915) dedicated his life to the study of tropical diseases, particularly yellow fever. At great personal risk, he discovered that the illness was transmitted by a mosquito of the genus *Stegomyia*, now named *Aedes Aegypti*. Finlay served as Cuba's Chief Health Officer during the administration of President Tomás Estrada Palma.

he announced that a constituent convention would be convened in Havana. The assembly would be composed of elected Cuban delegates. Their task would be to write a constitution, but one that would have two separate purposes. The first and obvious one was to set the basis for an independent Cuban government. The second was to determine the future of Cuban relations with the United States.

The inaugural session of the constituent convention was opened by Wood in November 1900. The delegates met for four months. They were inspired in their work by the example of the United States Constitution. The document drafted by the convention established a tripartite system of government with separate legislative, executive and judicial branches of power. The new constitution was ready on the eleventh of February 1901 and was ratified ten days later. Known as the Constitution of 1901, it remained in vigor until 1940.

The delegates had not been as successful in dealing with the second purpose of the constituent convention. Many of them correctly believed that a decision meant to regulate the future course of relations between Cuba and any foreign power did not fall under their jurisdiction. While these discussions were going on, an American Senator from Connecticut named Orville Platt attached a rider to the United States Army Appropriations Bill of 1901. Called the Platt Amendment, it established the basic conditions that had to be met before the United States would withdraw from Cuba.

The Platt Amendment had eight provisions. Cuba was prohibited from making any foreign treaties that might jeopardize its independence, in whichever way that could be interpreted. The struggling new nation was not allowed to incur public debts. All the measures taken by the United States during its intervention had to be ratified and implemented. Cuba had to make land available for the establishment of American naval bases. It was required not to make a similar arrangement with any other nation. The Isle of Pines was excluded from Cuba's national territory pending further discussions.[4] More serious was the provision that granted the United States the right to intervene in Cuba whenever it felt that the freedom and welfare of the population required it. A permanent treaty between Cuba and the United States had to be signed to formalize these provisions and to guarantee their proper enforcement.

4 The Isle of Pines is the largest of the thousands of islands and keys that surround Cuba. It lies some 50 kilometers from the south coast of Pinar del Río. In 1925, the United States recognized it as part of Cuba.

The Framboyan (Delonix Regia) or Royal Poinciana adds color to many Cuban squares. It was brought to the island from the East along with the sugar cane.

The rider was approved by the United States Congress and ratified by President McKinley. Cubans were dismayed. Accepting the Platt Amendment would turn Cuba into an American protectorate. Rejecting it would simply prolong their occupation of the island. In the end, the Platt Amendment was tolerated as the lesser of two evils. On the 12th of June 1901, it was adopted as an appendix to the new constitution. Cubans would quip that the Republic had been born with accute appendicitis.

The Platt Amendment caused great resentment in Cuba and was widely criticized in Latin America as evidence of the imperialist ambitions of the United States. It was abrogated by an international conference in 1934. Nevertheless, an American naval base remains at Guantánamo to this day.

With their work completed, the constituent convention was dissolved in October 1901. The next effort would be the election of a new president. The choice had narrowed down to three candidates. The first was General Máximo Gómez, who had been one of the most important commanders in both the Ten Years War and the War of Independence. He was the most popular choice, but he was 75 years old and refused the nomination. The second was Bartolomé Masó, who also withdrew from the race. The only remaining candidate was Tomás Estrada Palma. Elections were held in December 1901 and he was declared the winner. He had been living in the United States at that time.

Estrada Palma had been born in Bayamo and had taken part in the Ten Years War. The rebels had elected him president of the incipient republic in 1877. He had moved to the United States after the Pact of El Zanjón and had earned his living there as a schoolteacher. He had taken American citizenship, which he had to renounce to assume his office. His return to Cuba was marked by demonstrations of patriotic fervor. He landed in Oriente and visited Yara, the cradle of the independence movement, before traveling to Havana.

The first President of the Republic of Cuba was inaugurated on the 20th of May 1902. Estrada Palma was not a statesman. The main objective of his administration was to control the economy. The government was besieged by the veterans of the War of Independence, who demanded pensions and other types of compensation. Although Estrada Palma personally handled public finances with scrupulous honesty, his administration was plagued by rumors of favoritism in the handling of pension funds.

Estrada Palma successfully ran for reelection in 1905. However, the opposition Liberal Party accused him of fraud. Before he could start his second term, a revolt broke out under the leadership of one of his political rivals,

Detail of the inner courtyard of the Palacio del Segundo Cabo in Havana.

José Miguel Gómez. The situation grew very tense. Estrada Palma resigned and the government collapsed. Following the terms of the Platt Amendment, the American President, Theodore Roosevelt, decided to intervene. His Secretary of War, William Howard Taft, was dispatched to Cuba as provisionall governor.[5]

The second American intervention in Cuba began with Taft's arrival in Havana at the end of September 1906. It lasted for 27 months. Taft took only two weeks to negotiate a settlement and end the revolt. He was replaced by Edward Magoon, who had been the American governor of the Panama Canal Zone. Magoon acted as provisional governor from October 1906 until January 1908.

5   Taft became President of the United States in 1909.

Detail of the inner courtyard of the Palace of the Governors in Havana.

Magoon's two years in Cuba had constructive consequences for the island. He stimulated the development of agriculture and improved the highway system. A census was conducted under American supervision in 1907. It disclosed that the population had increased to slightly over two million inhabitants. The census was followed by a reorganization of the electoral registry. These last two measures were part of an effort to prepare the country for the coming elections, which would return the government to Cuban hands.

José Miguel Gómez became the second President of Cuba in 1909. He was followed in 1913 by Mario García Menocal, who had been the youngest general in the War of Independence. Cuba enjoyed a period of phenomenal prosperity during Menocal's two terms in office. The First World War had resulted in a marked increase in the price of sugar, which was the country's principal source of income.

Alfredo Zayas served as President from 1921 to 1925. He had been one of the delegates to the Constituent Convention of 1901. Zayas was a man of extensive learning who loved literature and wrote poetry. Unfortunately, the boom years of the First World War had come to an end. Cuba entered a phase of severe financial recession.

Gerardo Machado was elected to the first of his two terms as president in 1925. He was the first Cuban leader to exercise dictatorial powers. With the exception of Miguel Mariano Gómez, Ramón Grau San Martín and Carlos Prío Socarrás, the Cuban political scene has been dominated by dictators until the present time.

Index

142

Additional Reading

CARPENTIER, Alejo. *La Ciudad de las Columnas.* Havana, Editorial Letras Cubanas, 1982.

CHATELOIN, Felicia. *La Habana de Tácon.* Havana, Editorial Letras Cubanas, 1989.

COLUMBUS, Christopher. *Los Cuatro Viajes del Almirante y su Testamento.* Edited by Ignacio B. Anzoátegui. Madrid, Editorial Espasa-Calpe, 1964.

FERNANDEZ-ARMESTO, Felipe. *Columbus.* Oxford/New York, Oxford University Press, 1991.

GUERRA, Ramiro. *Manual de Historia de Cuba.* Havana, Instituto Cubano del Libro, 1971.

LANDSTRÖM, Björn. *Columbus.* New York, The Macmillan Company, 1967.

LLANES, Llilian. *Apuntes Para una Historia Sobre los Constructores Cubanos.* Havana, Editorial Letras Cubanas, 1985.

PORTUONDO DEL PRADO, Fernando. *Historia de Cuba.* Havana, Editorial Nacional de Cuba, 1965.

THOMAS, Hugh. *Cuba or the Pursuit of Freedom.* London, Eyre & Spottiswoode, 1971.

WEISS, Joaquín E. *La Arquitectura Colonial Cubana.* Havana, Editorial Pueblo y Educación, 1985.